Pork and Pineapple Curry
(Serves Four)

1 large Chopped Onion
40 g (1½ oz) Butter
450 g (1 lb) Leg or Pork, cubed
25 g (1 oz) Flour
1-2 tablespoons Curry Powder
1 × 200 g (8 oz) tin Pineapple Pieces
1 tablespoon Tomato Purée
50 g (2 oz) Sultanas
280 ml (½ pint) Water and Juice from pineapple
140 ml (¼ pint) Milk
Pinch of Salt
150 g (6 oz) Long grain rice

METHOD
1. Cook rice in lightly salted boiling water for 12 minutes.
2. Fry onions in butter until soft, then add pork and fry on all sides until lightly browned.
3. Stir in flour and curry powder, add remaining ingredients (except rice), bring to the boil and simmer, stirring continuously until meat is tender.
4. Season and pour into serving dish, surround with the freshly boiled rice and serve immediately.

SUGGESTED ACCOMPANIMENTS TO SERVE WITH CURRY
Mango Chutney   Sliced Cucumber   Sliced Bananas   Onion Rings   Tomato Slices   Coconut

What's Cooking?

What's Cooking?

A step-by-step guide

Jan Hopcraft

illustrated by

Sue Grant

J M Dent & Sons Ltd

CUNNINGHAME DIST. LIB.
Acc. No. C95186
CLASS No. J641.5

First published 1976
Text © Jan Hopcraft, 1976
Illustrations © J. M. Dent & Sons Ltd, 1976
All rights reserved. No part of this publication may be reproduced, stored in a retrieval system, or transmitted, in any form or by any means, electronic, mechanical, photocopying, recording or otherwise, without the prior permission of J. M. Dent & Sons Limited.

Printed in Great Britain by Biddles Ltd Guildford Surrey
and bound at the Aldine Press Letchworth Herts.
for J. M. Dent & Sons Limited
Aldine House Albemarle Street London

This book is set in 11pt IBM Theme

ISBN 0 460 06710 9

Contents

Taking Charge for the Day — 12
Menus for breakfast, lunch, tea and supper

Easy Menus for Lunch and Supper — 31
Toad-in-the-hole, cheese and onion flan, baked bananas, meringues and many other quick-to-make recipes

Casual Snacks for Hungry Friends — 54
Ideas for any time of the day, including barbecued hamburgers and frankfurters

Sweets and Biscuits to Eat or Give Away — 64
Recipes for fudge, peppermint creams and crunchy ginger biscuits—and ideas for gift-wrapping

Cakes for Special People — 71
Recipe for a basic cake with plenty of suggestions for alternative flavours and decorations—and a recipe for an Ice-Cream Birthday Cake

Vegetables — 80

Salads — 83

Index — 92

Oven Temperatures and Useful Measures — 94

Cooking is not at all difficult especially if you are just a little greedy and like eating. All you have to do is measure the ingredients carefully and read each recipe through thoroughly before you start so as to make sure you understand all the instructions. It is a great mistake to be careless. I once made a stupid error over the weight of garlic and ended up with thirty-two cloves instead of two. The result was disastrous, because garlic has a very strong flavour and if you eat it you smell of it for some time. After my muddle nobody wanted to come near me for days!

I hope that you will find the recipes in this book fun to make and delicious to eat.

Important: The spoon quantities given in this book are based on plastic measuring spoons. Level spoons have been used throughout unless otherwise stated.

The metrication working-party set up by the U.K. Federation for Education in Home Economics recommends that for convenience one ounce is converted as 25grams instead of the exact conversion figure of 28.35grams. For this reason you will find that recipes in this book give, for example, 4oz = 100grams.

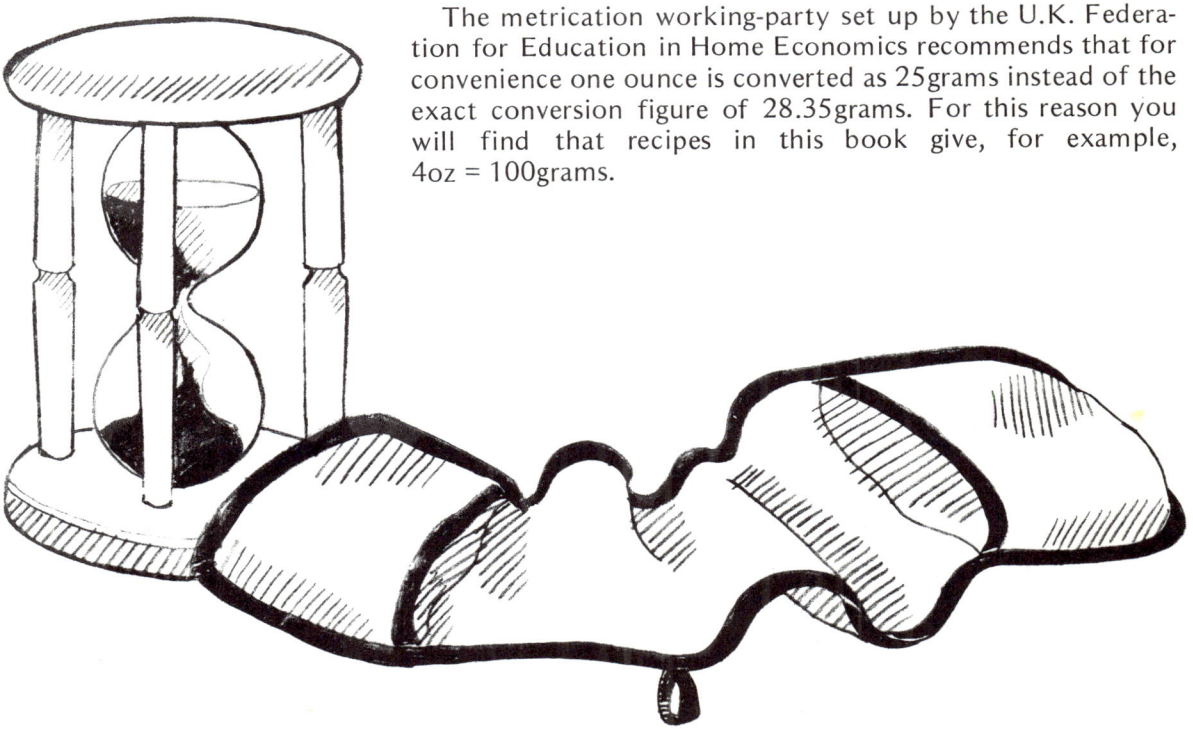

Taking Charge for the Day

Volunteering to cook all the meals for a day is opting for a lot of hard work. Nevertheless, it can be fun. Having established that you are taking charge it is important to make it clear that no one is allowed in the kitchen except by invitation. If well-meaning adults cannot resist trying to interfere, smile charmingly and hand them some onions to peel and chop. They will most probably become red-eyed and tear-streaked and you will have quietly made your point!

Meals have to be planned carefully. It isn't any good deciding on a menu of fudge, meringues, ice-cream, biscuits and a cake if you are taking charge for a day. The adults would undoubtedly decide to eat somewhere else or make their own meals. This would spoil the whole idea, and even you might long for a lettuce leaf as an escape from so much sugar and sweetness! Flavour, texture, protein and vitamin values aren't the only things to be considered either when planning a meal; colour is just as important. Imagine a meal of white fish, mashed potatoes, and cauliflower with a white sauce. It wouldn't look at all appetizing; but switch the cauliflower for peas and the dish becomes instantly attractive.

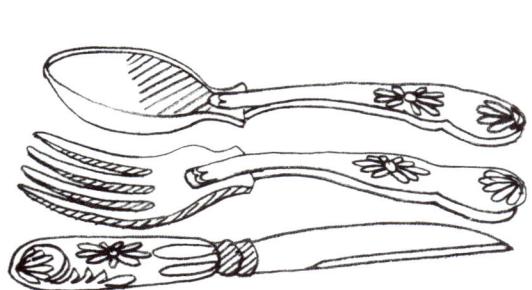

The table has to be laid correctly. Start by making a decoration for the centre of the table from flowers, fruit, coloured paper or anything else you can think of that looks cheerful. The only easy way to cope with the actual laying part is to go through the menu course by course to see that all the cutlery, plates, glasses and cups and saucers needed are on the table. The forks go on the left, the table mat in the middle, and the knives and spoons on the right with the glass or cup and saucer above. Remember that cutlery is used starting from the outside. Also, do not forget the extra table mats for hot dishes and the tea and coffee pots, as it is quite easy to make a mark on a polished table that will never come out. Remember, too, to work out what will be needed in the way of salt, pepper, sugar, bread, butter and water.

Kitchens can be dangerous, so as well as remembering to wash your hands before handling food because of germs, there are several safety points to be observed.

Saucepan handles, for instance, should always be turned in towards the stove but make sure they avoid another burner. If they stick out into the room they can easily be knocked off on to the floor.

Knives are often much sharper than they look, so always cut with the knife edge facing away from you or straight downwards.

Stoves and cooking pans can get very hot so have oven gloves or an oven cloth within easy reach. Hot food should be served on hot dishes, so protect your hands, otherwise you may be forced to drop a dish! In fact, make it a rule to wear oven gloves whenever you handle *anything* hot.

If you can, find a willing slave. The only snag to taking charge for a day is the washing and clearing up. If you leave the saucepans dirty, the stove covered with grease and bits of food, and the floor sprinkled with flour, the chances are that you won't be allowed the run of the kitchen again.

Just one more warning, if you burn or cut yourself go at once and find the nearest adult to give you first aid.

Menus for a Day

Check first to see that you have all the ingredients you need for the menus below.

Breakfast
Cereal or fruit juice
Eggs and bacon *or* boiled eggs   *pages 16, 17*
Toast   *page 17*
Coffee *or* tea   *pages 18, 19*

Lunch
Honey brown chicken   *page 20*
Vegetables in season   *page 80*
Iced syllabub or rhubarb or gooseberry snow   *pages 23, 24*

Afternoon Tea
Tea
Scones *or* chocolate biscuit cake   *pages 25, 26*

Supper
Onion soup   *page 27*
Kedgeree *or* spaghetti bolognese   *pages 45, 28*
Chocolate mandarin orange trifle   *page 30*

One good meal a day is quite enough for most people, so if you don't want to work flat out all day skip the cooked breakfast, afternoon tea, and the starter and pudding for supper.

All good cooks read through the recipe from beginning to end before they start. Your dish will be all the more delicious if you follow each instruction carefully.

The following time-table is intended to help you plan your day. It assumes that breakfast will be at 9, lunch at 13.00, afternoon tea at 16.30 and supper at 19.30.

Time Table

8.30	Lay the table for breakfast.
8.45	Cut the bread for toast, find the eggs and get out all the other ingredients and tools you will need. If you are cooking bacon start now, otherwise wait until people arrive looking hungry!
10.00	Make the chocolate biscuit cake for tea and the iced syllabub for lunch.
11.00	Prepare the vegetables for lunch and get the chicken ready for the oven. Start making the bread sauce.
11.40	Pre-heat the oven for the chicken (200°C, 400°F, Mark 6) and then lay the table for lunch.
11.50	Put the chicken in the oven. Cook the giblets for stock.
12.05	Make the rhubarb or gooseberry snow.
12.15	Turn down the oven (180°C, 350°F, Mark 4).
12.25	Make the basic gravy.
12.15–12.45	Bring the water for the vegetables to boiling point. The timing depends on what you are cooking (*page 80*). Put the water for the potatoes on at 12.20.
12.45	Drain the potatoes and put in a dish to keep warm. This will save you dishing up everything at the last minute!
12.50	Finish making the bread sauce.
13.00	Switch off the oven and take the chicken out. Finish making the gravy. Drain the second vegetable.
15.00	Make the scones for tea and the mandarin orange trifle for supper.
16.15	Lay the table for tea.
16.25	Make the tea.
18.10	Start making the onion soup.
18.30	Lay the table for supper.
18.45	Make the sauce for the spaghetti bolognese or make the kedgeree. Keep the latter warm in a covered basin sitting over a pan of simmering water.
19.00	Put the water on to boil for the spaghetti.
19.25	Drain the spaghetti.

One more lot of washing up and you are through for the day!

Eggs and Bacon

Ingredients
25g (1oz) fat
4 bacon rashers
4 eggs

Serves 4

Tools
frying pan, spoon, fishslice, cup, kitchen scissors or sharp knife, fork, chopping board, plates, oven gloves

Method

1. Remove the bacon rind, preferably with kitchen scissors as this is the safest method. Or lay the bacon on a chopping board and use a sharp knife.
2. Put the bacon in the frying pan. Try to see it doesn't overlap, but if it does, arrange it so that fat covers lean. Add the bacon rind.
3. Cook the bacon in a frying pan on a low heat on the stove. You can always increase the heat later if you think the bacon isn't cooking fast enough.
4. Put the plates in a very cool oven (110°C, 225°F, Mark ¼) to warm.
5. Allow the bacon to cook for 5 minutes on each side, turning with a fork. If you are using a non-stick pan be very careful not to scratch it.
6. *While the bacon is cooking make the coffee if you are using the 'real' ground variety.*
7. Take the hot plates out of the oven.
8. Remove the pan from the heat and, using a fork, take the bacon from the pan and put a rasher on each plate.
9. Put the plates back in the oven.
10. *Start making the toast.*
11. Put the frying pan back on the stove, add the extra fat, and heat it for 1 minute before cooking the eggs.
12. Crack an eggshell sharply in its middle on the edge of the cup.
13. Gently place the egg in the frying pan slightly off centre. With a spoon try to gather the white round the yolk. When the white has set you can repeat the process with the next egg. More than 2 eggs are difficult to cook in one pan.
14. Cook the eggs for 2-3 minutes and spoon fat over them from time to time. If you like your eggs 'sunny side down' turn them over with a fishslice just before they are cooked.
15. Take a plate with bacon on it out of the oven.
16. Remove an egg from the pan by sliding a fishslice gently under it. Be careful, as they break very easily. Transfer the egg to the bacon plate by letting it slide gently off the fishslice.
17. Return the bacon and the egg to the oven to keep warm until needed, but do not attempt to keep the egg hot for long.

It may cheer you up to know that if you can cook perfect bacon and eggs, then the chances are that you will find everything else in this book easy to do!

Boiled Eggs

Ingredients Serves 4
4 eggs

Tools
saucepan, tablespoon, egg cups, oven gloves

Method
1. Put enough water in a pan to cover the number of eggs you plan to boil, and bring the water to the boil on the stove. *Start making the toast at this point and also the tea or coffee. Don't cook the eggs until people arrive for breakfast.*
2. Put the eggs gently into the boiling water with the aid of a spoon.
3. If the water appears to be just steaming instead of gently bubbling turn up the heat. Be careful to turn the heat down again if the water bubbles hard, otherwise the eggs will crack.
4. Cook for 4-5 minutes. It is usual to ask people how long they would like their egg to cook. Fresh farm eggs take about 1 minute longer than ones which are more then a few days old. (Hard-boiled eggs take 10 minutes.)
5. Take the pan off the heat and immediately remove the eggs with a spoon and place them in the egg cups. Be careful again about the steam, and wear an oven glove.

If the eggs are stored in a refrigerator try to take them out in time for them to warm a little before cooking as this will help prevent them from cracking.

Toast

Ingredients Serves 4
4 slices of bread

Tools
bread knife, board

Method
1. If you don't have an electric toaster light the gas grill. If you use an electric grill, switch it on for 2 minutes before you put the toast on otherwise it will take ages to brown and harden in the process.
2. Cut the bread, but don't cut yourself!
3. Put the slices of bread under the grill.
4. Watch carefully and turn once they are brown; watch the second side brown too.

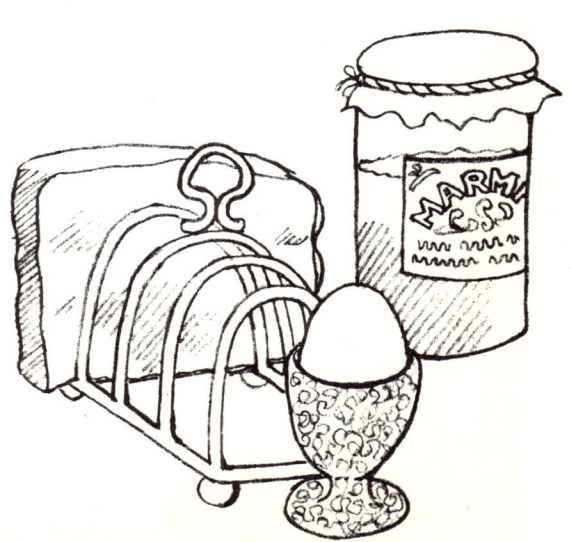

'Real' Coffee

makes 6 teacupfuls

Ingredients   Serves 4
6 tablespoons ground coffee
1 litre (1¾ pints) water
250ml (½ pint) milk

Tools
kettle, heat-proof jug, small mesh strainer or tea strainer, tablespoon, small saucepan, oven gloves

There are many methods for making 'real' coffee, but one of the easiest and best is to make it in a heat-proof jug. Find out how much water the jug holds, (most jugs have the number of litres or pints marked on the bottom), but if in doubt you can easily check with a measuring cup or milk bottle full of water.

Method
1. Bring the water to the boil in a kettle.
2. Warm the coffee jug with a little of the boiling water, then empty it out.
3. Put the ground coffee in the pot and pour on the boiling water.
4. Allow to stand in a warm place for 5 minutes.
5. While the coffee is standing, heat the milk on the stove, but do not allow it to boil.
6. Using a strainer either pour the coffee into the cups or into another warmed jug.
7. Either pour the milk into a warmed jug or add to the coffee in the cups.

'Instant' Coffee

Allow the following:
1 teaspoon 'instant' coffee per teacup
2 teaspoons 'instant' coffee per mug
4 teaspoons 'instant' coffee per ½ litre
   (1 pint)

Bring the water to boiling point, or a mixture of half water and half milk. If you are using water and milk together heat until very hot but try not to let the mixture actually boil. Pour the liquid over the coffee and serve it at once if you have made it in a cup. Coffee in a jug can be kept hot in a warm place.

Tea

makes 6 teacupfuls

Ingredients
4 teaspoons of tea or 3 teabags
1 litre (1¾ pints) water

Serves 4

Tools
kettle, teapot, teaspoon, oven gloves

Method
1 Boil the water in a kettle.
2 Warm the teapot with a little of the boiling water, then empty it out.
3 Put the tea in the teapot.
4 Bring the water to the boil once more.
5 Pour the water quickly but carefully on to the tea, taking care not to pour it over yourself!
6 Leave to stand for 5 minutes.

Honey Brown Chicken

Ingredients Serves 4
1 roasting chicken (about 1½kg/3¼lb)
50g (2oz) butter
1 tablespoon golden syrup
Salt and pepper

Tools
roasting pan, small saucepan, knife, 2 tablespoons, tinfoil or greaseproof paper, fork, fishslice, serving dish, oven gloves

Method

1. Pre-heat the oven to fairly hot (200°C, 400°F, or Mark 6).
2. Remove the giblets from inside the chicken—these may be in a plastic bag. If the chicken is a frozen one make sure it has completely defrosted before cooking.
3. Put the giblets, without the bag, in a pan with a pinch of salt and a shake of pepper and cover with water. Set the pan on the stove and simmer slowly on a low heat for at least half an hour, adding more water if necessary. Use as stock for gravy.
4. Put the chicken in a roasting pan. Spread the butter over the breast and legs. Spoon over the golden syrup and sprinkle with salt and pepper. It is a good idea to put the tin of syrup near the stove before you use it to make the syrup more pliable, or use a warm spoon.
5. Check that the oven is hot enough and then, using oven gloves, put the chicken on the middle shelf.
6. After 20 minutes lower the oven temperature to moderate to fairly hot: (180°-190°C, 350°-375°F, Mark 4-5).
7. Cook for about an hour—a chicken which has been frozen may take longer than a fresh one.
8. Spoon fat over the bird every 20 minutes, this is known as basting. Take great care not to burn yourself when spooning the fat from the bottom of the roasting pan.
9. When the chicken has turned golden brown cover the breast with greaseproof paper or tinfoil.
10. When it is cooked remove the chicken from the pan with the help of a fork and a fishslice and place on a serving dish. Switch off the oven and put the chicken back in it—leave the door slightly open otherwise the serving dish may crack!
11. Gently tip the roasting pan up on one side and spoon the top layer of fat into a container; never pour fat straight down the sink as it will block up the drain. Add the prepared basic gravy mix, *page 22*, to the remaining liquid in the pan.
12. Heat the gravy in the pan on the stove until it bubbles. Pour the gravy into a heatproof jug.

If you feel that preparing vegetables would be the last straw, serve with salad, *page 83* and French bread and butter. Instructions for cooking vegetables appear on *pages 80, 81, 82*.

Bread Sauce

Ingredients   Serves 4
3 teacupfuls (about 6 slices bread) fresh white breadcrumbs
1 large onion
20 cloves
375ml (¾ pint) milk
Pepper and ¼ teaspoon salt

Tools
grater or blender, bread knife, teaspoon, wooden spoon, measuring cup, small saucepan, oven gloves

If you are in a hurry use packet bread sauce, in which case follow the instructions on the packet.

Method
1. Make the breadcrumbs, *page 48.*
2. Peel the onion and stick the cloves into it.
3. Put the onion and milk together in a saucepan.
4. Put the saucepan on the stove on a low heat, and bring the milk very slowly to the boil. Watch carefully otherwise it may boil over.
5. Once the milk has boiled remove the saucepan from the stove and add the breadcrumbs, salt and several shakes of pepper. Leave to stand for at least 20 minutes.
6. Five minutes before you need the sauce remove the onion, put the saucepan with the bread sauce in it back on the stove and bring it to the boil. Turn the heat down and simmer. Stir frequently as bread sauce can very easily stick to the bottom of the pan and burn. If it becomes too thick add a little more milk.

Basic Gravy

Ingredients   Serves 4
250ml (½ pint) water or giblet stock
½ a chicken- or beef-stock cube
2 teaspoons flour
1 teaspoon Worcestershire sauce
Few drops gravy browning
1 bay leaf

Tools
small saucepan, 2 teaspoons, measuring cup, wooden spoon, oven gloves

Use a chicken-stock cube when you are making gravy for a chicken and a beef-stock cube for a dish like toad-in-the-hole. If you like thick gravy add another 1-2 teaspoons of flour.

Method
1. Put the flour in a basin and blend in a little of the water to make a smooth paste. Add the rest of the water, the bay leaf, Worcestershire sauce and the stock cube crumbled in small pieces.

2. Cook the mixture in a saucepan on the stove and stir all the time until it boils and thickens. Add a few drops of gravy browning. Turn the heat down and simmer for about 3 minutes. Take the pan off the stove and leave the basic gravy on one side until you want to reheat it. Remember to remove the bay leaf before serving.

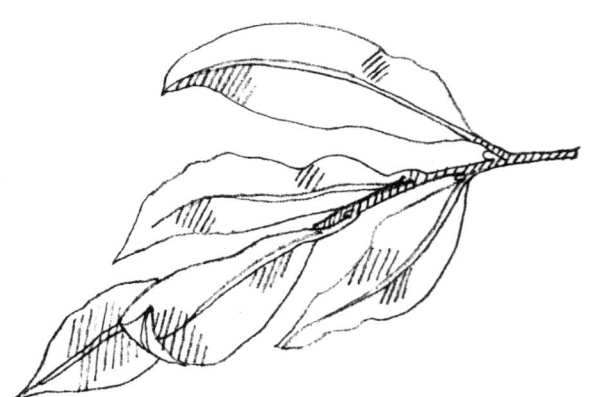

Bay leaves, fresh or dried, are used frequently in cooking. They are placed whole in soups, stews and casseroles and should always be removed before serving. They have a fairly distinctive flavour and one leaf is generally enough to use at a time. They come from the bay tree which is cultivated almost as much for ornamental as for culinary purposes.

Iced Syllabub

Ingredients Serves 4
125ml (¼ pint) double cream
2 egg whites
100g (¼lb) icing sugar
Juice of 1 orange and 1 lemon
 to make 125ml (¼ pint)

Tools
lemon squeezer, egg beater, 2 basins, measuring cup, metal spoon, soufflé dish or ice tray

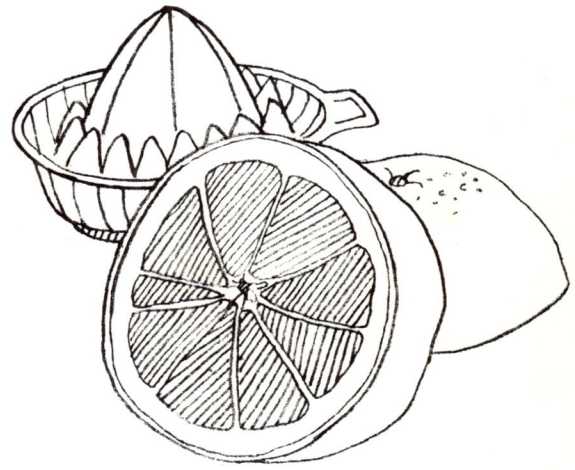

Method
1. Cut the orange and lemon in half and squeeze out the juice with a lemon squeezer. Measure the juice to see that you have not got more than 125ml (¼ pint). It does not matter if there is less juice than this.

2. Put the cream, fruit juice and icing sugar together in a bowl. Whisk with an egg beater until the mixture thickens and looks like soft whipped cream.

3. Separate the yolks from the whites of the eggs. Put the whites in a basin and the yolks in a small covered container to keep for another recipe.

4. Beat the egg whites until they are stiff with a clean, dry egg beater.

5. Fold the egg whites into the cream mixture with a metal spoon. Cut through to the bottom of the bowl each time pretending you are drawing a circle.

6. Spoon the mixture into an ice tray or soufflé dish, first making sure the dish fits into the ice-making compartment of the refrigerator.

7. The iced syllabub will be ready to eat in 2½ hours but can be left for several days. It will harden if kept and turn into ice-cream.

Rhubarb and Gooseberry Snow

Ingredients   Serves 4
1 tin (350ml/⅝ pint) evaporated milk
400g (about 1lb) rhubarb*
1 tablespoon lemon juice
4 tablespoons sugar
4 tablespoons water
Few drops red edible food colouring

*Gooseberries can be used instead of rhubarb, top and tail them and cook without the lemon juice for about 10 minutes until soft. Add a few drops of green edible colouring instead of red.

Tools
tin opener, 2 basins, chopping board, knife, saucepan, spoon, egg beater, tablespoon, wooden spoon, sieve, oven gloves

Method
1. Cut the rhubarb into 2½cm/1in pieces.
2. Put the rhubarb in a saucepan with the lemon juice, sugar and water.
3. Put the saucepan on the stove and cook slowly until the rhubarb is mushy. This will take 15-20 minutes. Stir occasionally.
4. While the rhubarb is cooking open the tin of evaporated milk and pour it into a basin. Whip with an egg beater for 5 minutes until it thickens—you may find your arm becomes rather tired!
5. Remove the saucepan from the stove. Set the sieve over a basin and rub the rhubarb through with a spoon, or use a blender.
6. Mix the rhubarb and whipped evaporated milk together.
7. Add a little red edible food colouring, 1 drop at a time, and stir thoroughly. This pudding should be a delicate pink colour.
8. Put the rhubarb snow in a glass dish and serve with granulated sugar if you like a crunch topping.

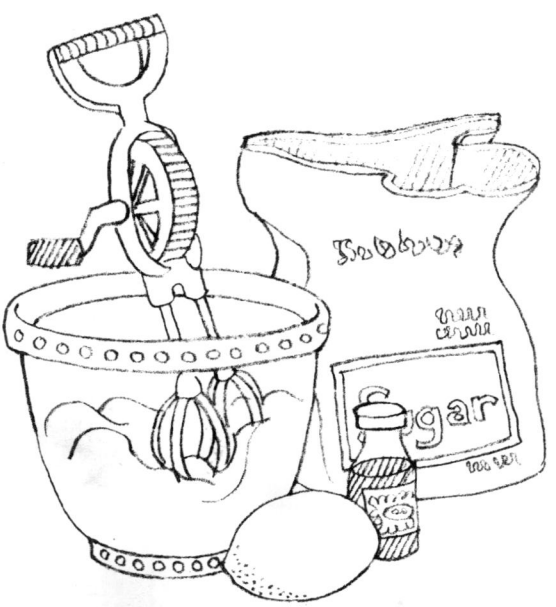

If there is any rhubarb snow over, place it in a tray in the ice-making section of the refrigerator where it will turn into ice-cream.

Scones

Ingredients — Makes about 10
- 75g (3oz) margarine or butter
- 200g (8oz) plain flour
- 2 level teaspoons baking powder
- 125ml (¼ pint) milk
- 2 tablespoons sugar, only essential if you like sweet scones
- 4 tablespoons sultanas, also not essential
- Pinch salt

Tools
sieve, mixing basin, blunt knife, pastry board, rolling pin, tablespoon, teaspoon, baking tray, pastry cutter, wire cake rack, fishslice, measuring cup, buttered paper, oven gloves

Method

1. Pre-heat the oven to very hot (230°C, 450°F, Mark 8).
2. Sieve the flour into a mixing basin and add the baking powder and salt and sugar if required.
3. Cut the margarine or butter into small pieces and put into the basin with the flour.
4. Rub the fat into the flour by rubbing it between your thumbs and the tips of your fingers. Try and avoid getting flour on the palms of your hands.
5. When the mixture begins to look like breadcrumbs, add the sultanas. Then make a hollow in the centre by pushing the mixture evenly round the side of the basin.
6. Pour three-quarters of the milk into the hollow and stir it into the flour mixture with a knife to form a soft but not sticky dough. If it is too dry to hold together add a little more milk.
7. Put some flour on the pastry board. Place the dough on the board and with a rolling pin, roll it out to a thickness of about 2cm/¾in.
8. Either cut the scone mixture into triangles with a knife or into rounds with a pastry cutter.
9. Grease the baking tray with a little butter or margarine.
10. Put the scones on the baking tray.
11. Place on the middle shelf in the oven and cook for about 13 minutes until the scones feel firm.
12. Take the scones out of the oven. Remove them from the baking tray with a fishslice and put them on a wire cake rack to cool.

Chocolate Biscuit Cake

Ingredients
100g (¼lb) butter
200g (½lb) broken sweet biscuits, preferably digestive
100g (¼lb) chocolate
3 tablespoons chocolate spread or golden syrup
4-6 glacé cherries for decoration, though these are not essential
For a richer cake double the quantity of butter

Tools
rolling pin, plastic bag, knife, saucepan, tablespoon, flan tin (about 17½cm/7in diameter), wooden spoon, meat plate, buttered paper, oven gloves

Method

1 Break the chocolate into small pieces.

2 Put the biscuits in a plastic bag and crush them with a rolling pin, until the larger pieces are no more than about 1¼cm/½in square.

3 Place the butter, chocolate and chocolate spread or syrup in a saucepan and cook on the stove over a low heat to melt. Stir and, when the mixture has completely melted, remove the saucepan from the stove.

4 Put the broken biscuits in the saucepan and stir thoroughly so that they are well covered with the chocolate mixture.

5 Grease a 17½cm/7in flan tin with a piece of buttered paper. The tin should preferably have a moveable bottom.

6 Put the biscuit mixture into the flan tin and sit it on a meat plate. Cut the cherries in half and decorate the cake. Leave in a refrigerator or other very cool place to set. Turn out of the tin before serving.

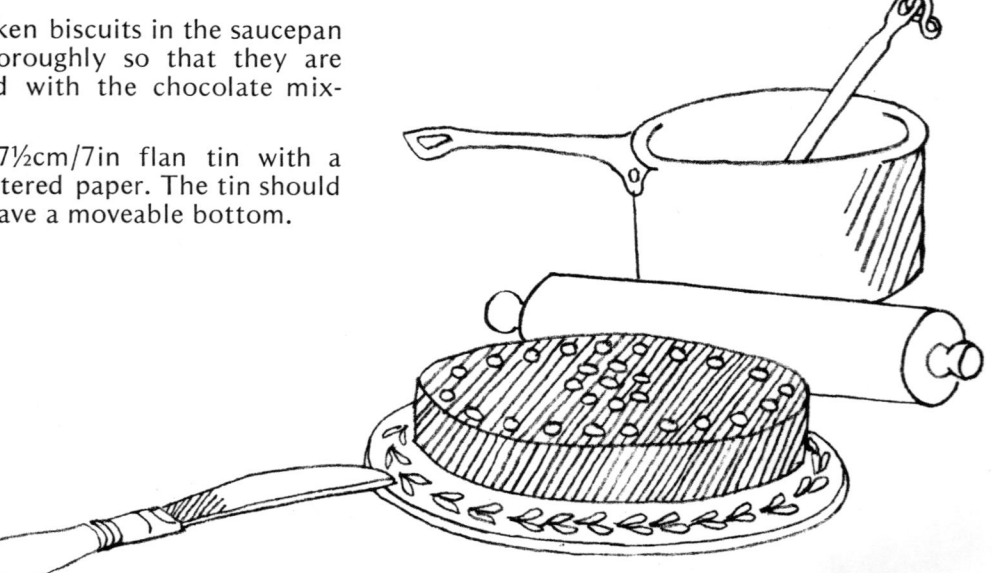

Onion Soup

Ingredients　　　　　　Serves 4
400g (1lb) onions
1 litre (1¾ pints) water
1 beef-stock cube
35g (1½oz) butter or margarine
1 teaspoon sugar
1 large slice of bread
25g (1oz) Cheddar cheese
Pinch of salt and pepper

Tools
knife, chopping board, fireproof casserole or saucepan and ovenproof dish, wooden spoon, grater, teaspoon, oven gloves

Method

1. Peel the onions and cut them in very fine slices.
2. Melt the butter or margarine in a fireproof casserole or saucepan on a low heat.
3. Put the onions in the casserole or saucepan and cover it with a lid. Turn the heat to very low and stew the onions for 20 minutes. Stir from time to time and make sure that the onions do not cook too fast and burn.
4. Pour in the water. Crumble the stock cube with your fingers, or chop with a knife, and add this to the water and onions.
5. Turn up the heat and bring the soup to the boil. Taste, taking care not to burn your tongue, add the sugar, salt and pepper, and then taste again. If you have been using a saucepan pour the soup slowly and carefully into an ovenproof dish.
6. Put the casserole or ovenproof dish in a cool oven (140°C, 275°F, Mark 1) for 50 minutes.
7. Toast the slice of bread and cut it into four *page 17*.
8. Grate the cheese and put a small mound on each piece of toast.
9. When the casserole has been in the oven for 30 minutes take the lid off and place the toast and cheese in the soup. Cook for a further 20 minutes and then serve.

Spaghetti Bolognese

(For Kedgeree see *page 45*)

Ingredients Serves 4

Sauce
400g (1lb) minced meat
1 onion
1 tin (396g/14oz) tomatoes
4 tablespoons concentrated tomato paste
1 tablespoon flour
1 tablespoon basil
2 bay leaves
1 tablespoon Worcestershire sauce
½ beef-stock cube
125ml (¼ pint) water
1 tablespoon cooking oil
Pepper and ¼ teaspoon salt
Grated Parmesan or Cheddar cheese (not essential)

Spaghetti
200g (8oz) spaghetti
1½ litres (2½ pints) water
1 tablespoon cooking oil
¼ teaspoon salt

Tools
tin opener, chopping board, wooden spoon, knife, large frying pan with a lid, or a saucepan, tablespoon, teaspoon, measuring cup, fork, sieve, saucepan, oven gloves

Method
Sauce
1. Peel the onion and chop it finely.
2. Heat the oil for about 1 minute in a frying pan on the stove.
3. Add the onion, stir, then cover with a saucepan lid and cook slowly for about 5 minutes. Look to see that the onion is not browning. If it is, turn down the heat.
4. Add the flour and stir it in well. Add the minced meat and stir it with a fork to break it all up. Cook slowly for 5 minutes.
5. Pour in the water and add the stock cube, crumbled in small pieces, the basil, bay leaves, Worcestershire sauce and the concentrated tomato paste. Stir again thoroughly.
6. Open the tin of tomatoes and add them to the mixture in the frying pan. Also add salt and pepper, taste and add more if necessary.
7. Simmer the sauce slowly for 20 minutes stirring from time to time. *At this point start cooking the spaghetti (see below).* If the sauce looks too thin turn the heat up and cook quickly for a few more minutes stirring all the time.

Spaghetti

1 Put the water in a saucepan and bring it to the boil on the stove. Add the salt.

2 Gently lower the spaghetti into the water taking great care not to burn yourself. Spaghetti becomes flexible in hot water so you will be able to slide it around the edge of the saucepan until it is all covered with water.

3 Add the cooking oil which will help to stop the spaghetti sticking together. Separate it with a fork while it is cooking.

4 Simmer and cook for 20-25 minutes. Test by cutting a small piece off with a fork and tasting it. Be careful not to burn your tongue!

5 Remove the pan from the stove and pour the spaghetti into a sieve to drain it.

To serve, divide the spaghetti between the plates and spoon the sauce on top, first removing the bay leaves. Sprinkle with grated Parmesan or Cheddar cheese.

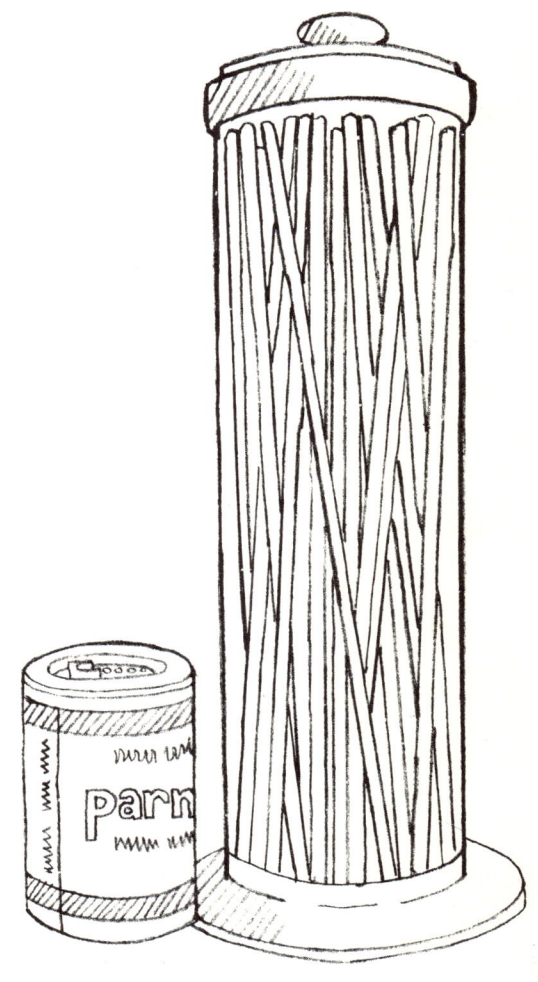

Basil originally came from India, but it is hardy enough to be grown outside in England. Sweet basil is the variety most frequently dried and the leaves and flowers are used in cooking. This herb is more pungent fresh but when dried still keeps its flavour. Basil is used a great deal in Italian and Greek cooking and goes particularly well with dishes containing cooked tomatoes as well as with meat and chicken.

Chocolate Mandarin Orange Trifle

Ingredients   Serves 4
1 150g (6oz) chocolate swiss roll
125ml (¼ pint) double cream
1 tin (312g/11oz) mandarin oranges
2 squares of grated chocolate for decoration

Tools
tin opener, serving bowl, chopping board, knife, spoon, basin, egg beater, grater

Method
1. Cut the swiss roll in thin slices, ½cm/¼in thick, and arrange them in layers in the bowl.
2. Open the tin of mandarins and cover the swiss roll slices with the juice and fruit.
3. Put the cream in a basin and whip it with an egg beater until it is thick.
4. With a spoon spread the cream over the orange and swiss roll mixture.
5. Sprinkle the grated chocolate over the top and leave to stand for at least an hour.

Easy Menus for Lunch and Supper

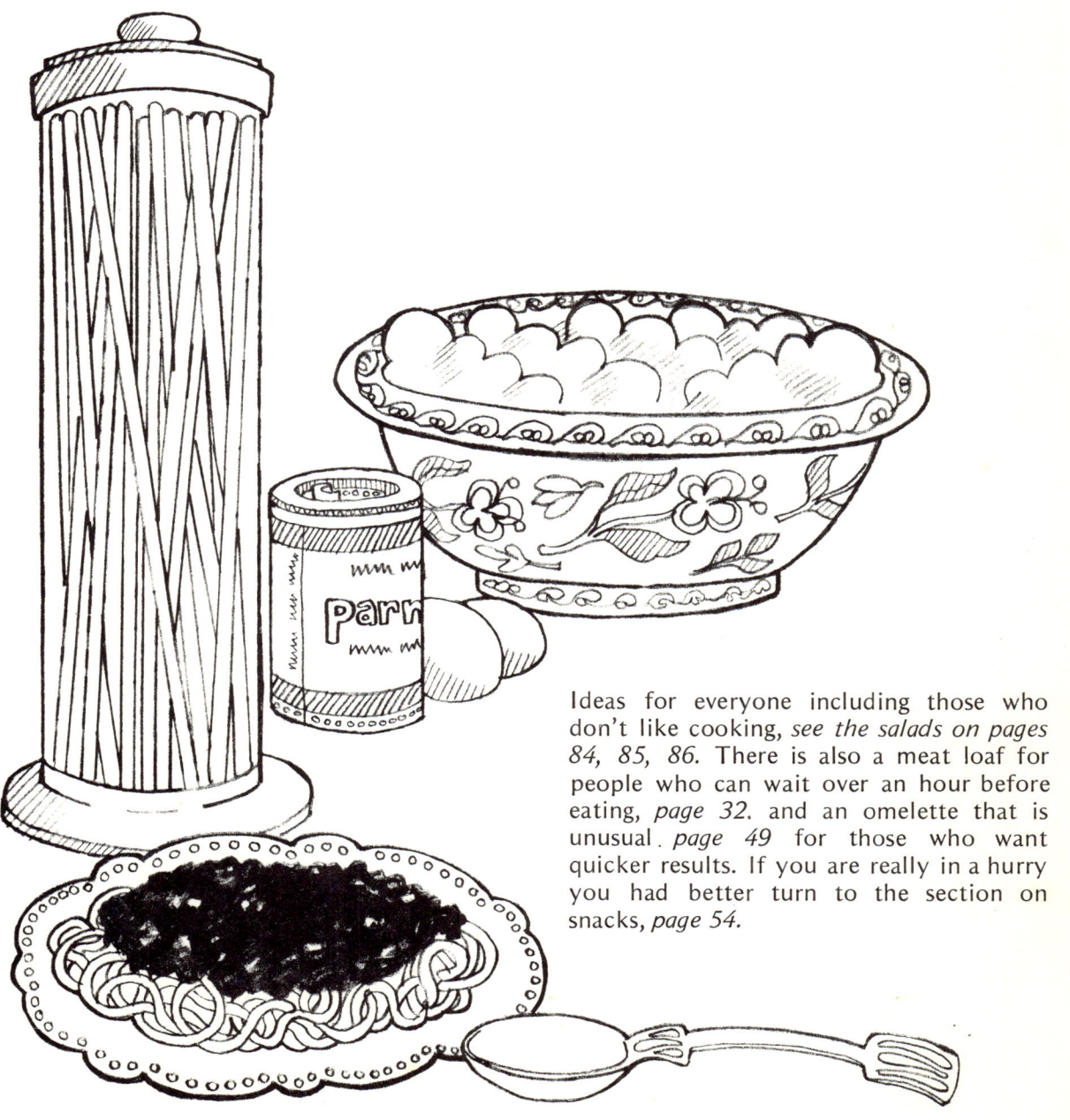

Ideas for everyone including those who don't like cooking, *see the salads on pages 84, 85, 86.* There is also a meat loaf for people who can wait over an hour before eating, *page 32.* and an omelette that is unusual *. page 49* for those who want quicker results. If you are really in a hurry you had better turn to the section on snacks, *page 54.*

Meat Loaf

Ingredients   Serves 4
250g (8oz) sausage-meat
250g (8oz) best minced beef
1½ teacupfuls fresh breadcrumbs
   (about 3 slices of bread) *page 48*
1 medium sized onion
1 egg
3 sprigs parsley
1 tablespoon tomato paste
1 tablespoon Worcestershire sauce
1 teaspoon basil
1 tablespoon cooking oil
Pinch of thyme
Salt and pepper

Tools
grater, blender, knife, chopping board, frying pan, mixing basin, small basin, tablespoon, teaspoon, fork, wooden spoon, 400g/1lb bread tin or other oven-proof container, buttered paper, oven gloves

Method

1. Peel the onion and chop it very finely. Also chop the parsley.

2. Heat the oil slowly in a frying pan on the stove for about 1 minute.

3. Pre-heat the oven to fairly hot (190°C, 375°F, Mark 5).

4. Cook the onion slowly in the frying pan for 5 minutes. Stir it occasionally. Turn the heat down if it starts looking brown.

5. Put the onion, sausage-meat, minced beef, breadcrumbs, parsley, tomato paste, Worcestershire sauce, basil and thyme in a mixing basin. Mix all these ingredients together with the salt and a shake of pepper. This is hard work!

6. Break the egg into a small basin, and beat it with a fork.

7. Add the beaten egg to the meat and stir thoroughly.

8. Grease a 400g/1lb bread tin with butter or margarine.

9. Put the mixture into it and smooth the surface with a spoon. Put in the oven and cook for 1 hour. Allow to cool for 5 minutes and then run a knife round the edge of the tin before turning out.

Meat loaf can be eaten hot with potatoes and a green vegetable or cold with a green salad; it makes a useful picnic dish.

Thyme has a strong, dominating flavour and it is important to use only a little at a time. Although it came originally from the Mediterranean it grows quite well in England and is used both fresh and dried. It goes very well with meat dishes and is often used in bread stuffings.

Meringues

Makes 8 halves

Ingredients Serves 4
2 large eggs
8 level tablespoons castor or icing sugar
125ml (¼ pint) double cream
Pinch of salt
Butter for greaseproof paper

Method
1. Cover the baking tray with a piece of lightly buttered greaseproof paper.
2. Separate the whites from the yolks of the eggs. Keep the yolks in a covered cup to use for mayonnaise etc.
3. Put the egg whites in a basin and add a pinch of salt.
4. Whisk the whites with an egg beater until they are stiff enough to form peaks.
5. Shake in half the sugar, a tablespoonful at a time, and whisk the white after each spoonful of sugar has been added.
6. Using a metal spoon fold in the rest of the sugar, again adding it a tablespoonful at a time.
7. Spoon the meringue mixture on to the baking tray with a dessert spoon to form 8 small mounds.
8. Put in a very cool oven (110°C, 225°F, Mark ¼) and cook until the meringues feel firm and can be easily removed from the paper. This will take about 1¼ hours. If they start browning lower the heat.
9. Place the meringues on a wire rack until completely cool.
10. Put the cream in a basin and whip it until it is stiff. Use it to sandwich the meringues together in pairs.

Tools
basin, egg beater, tablespoon, metal dessert spoon, baking tray, greaseproof paper, wire cake rack, oven gloves

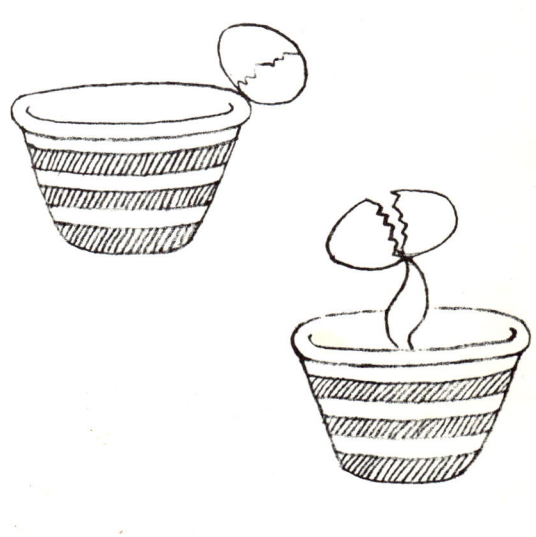

Coffee Crumble
If the meringues do not look as perfect as you would like, or you feel like something different, you can break them into small pieces about the size of walnuts. Then about an hour before the meal add 2 teaspoons of coffee essence to the whipped cream, mix well and stir in the meringue pieces. This makes a delicious pudding.

Cheese and Onion Flan

Ingredients
200ml (⅜ pint) milk, about 1 teacupful
3 eggs
100g (4oz) grated cheese
1 small onion
25g (1oz) butter or margarine
Salt and pepper
190-225g (7½-9oz) shortcrust pastry (frozen can be used)

Serves 4

Tools
grater, sandwich or flan tin, frying pan and lid, basin, tablespoon, teaspoon, wooden spoon, chopping board, sharp knife, oven gloves

Method

1. Prepare the pastry flan case, *page 50*.
2. Peel the onion and cut it in very thin slices, taking care not to cut your fingers.
3. Melt the butter or margarine in the frying pan on a low heat until it bubbles a little.
4. Put the onion slices into the frying pan and cover with a lid, and cook them very slowly for 8 minutes. If the onion starts to turn brown, lower the heat.
5. Remove the pan from the heat and spread the onion slices over the bottom of the flan case.
6. Pre-heat the oven to fairly hot (190°C, 375°F, Mark 5).
7. Break the eggs into the basin. Add the milk and beat lightly with a wooden spoon.
8. Grate the cheese and add it to the egg mixture.
9. Add salt and pepper and beat the mixture for half a minute before pouring it into the flan case.
10. Put the cheese and onion pie in the middle shelf in the oven and cook for 30 minutes, or until the egg sets.
11. Remove from the oven and allow to cool for 2 or 3 minutes before cutting.

Serve with a green salad, peas or beans.

Easy menus for lunch and supper

Oranges in Syrup

Ingredients
4 small oranges
100g (4oz) sugar
125ml (¼ pint) water

Serves 4

Tools
chopping board, sharp knife, saucepan, serving bowl, spoon, oven gloves

The coloured skin of an orange or lemon is correctly known as the zest.

Method
1. Taking great care not to cut yourself peel the oranges as you would an apple and try to remove the skin in one piece. Cut just under the pith through to the juicy orange. Hold the orange over the serving bowl while you do this to catch the juice.
2. Put the peeled oranges in the serving bowl until you are ready to slice them.
3. Put the sugar, water and the skin of one orange in a saucepan.
4. Put the saucepan on the stove and bring the sugar and water to the boil. Simmer for 20 minutes. Stir from time to time.
5. While the syrup is cooking take the oranges out of the bowl one at a time and cut them in thin slices on a chopping board. Put the slices and any more juice back in the serving dish.
6. Remove the saucepan from the stove and cool the syrup.
7. Then remove the orange skin from the cooled syrup and pour the syrup over the orange slices.

Ham with Bananas

Ingredients   Serves 4
4 small bananas
4 slices ham (about 100g/4oz)

Sauce
100g (4oz) grated cheese
250ml (½ pint) milk
2 tablespoons flour
25g (1oz) butter or margarine
Pepper and ¼ teaspoon salt

Topping
2 tablespoons dried breadcrumbs *page 48*
25g (1oz) butter or margarine

Tools
knife, saucepan, grater, teaspoon, tablespoon, wooden spoon, casserole, measuring cup, oven gloves

Method
Sauce
1. Melt the butter or margarine in a saucepan over a low heat on the stove.
2. Remove the saucepan from the stove and slowly stir in the flour and add the salt and two shakes of pepper.
3. Re-heat and cook this mixture, which is called a 'roux', until it bubbles and begins to change colour slightly.
4. Take the pan off the stove once more and very slowly stir in the milk making sure there are no lumps.
5. Put the saucepan back on the stove again and stir the mixture without stopping until it thickens. (If the worst happens and your sauce becomes lumpy you can press it through a sieve. This doesn't entirely save the sauce, but it helps!)
6. Add the cheese and cook for 2-3 minutes.

Ham with bananas
7. Peel the bananas and wrap each one in a slice of ham.
8. Put the bananas in an open casserole and pour the sauce over them.

Topping
9. Sprinkle on the breadcrumbs. Cut the butter into about 6 pieces and put these on top of the breadcrumbs.
10. Put the casserole under the grill and cook until the breadcrumbs look crisp and brown—this will take about 5 minutes.

Serve with spinach or green peas or beans.

Ginger Snap Slices

Ingredients
50g (2oz) butter
50g (2oz) demerara sugar
65g (2½oz)/3 tablespoons golden syrup
50g (2oz) flour
1 teaspoon powdered ginger
125ml (¼ pint) double cream for filling

Serves 4

Tools
saucepan, teaspoon, tablespoon, 2 baking trays, wire cake rack, fishslice, egg beater, basin, wooden spoon, buttered paper, oven gloves

Method
1. Pre-heat the oven to moderate (170°-180°C, 325°F, Mark 3-4).
2. Melt the butter in a saucepan over a low heat on the stove.
3. Remove the saucepan from the stove and add the sugar, golden syrup, flour and powdered ginger. Mix these ingredients well together.
4. Grease 2 baking trays with a little margarine.
5. Divide the mixture into 8 and space out 4 spoonfuls on each tray. It is important to leave plenty of room as the mixture will spread when it gets hot.
6. Put the trays on shelves near the middle of the oven and cook the ginger snap slices until they are a rich, golden brown. This will take about 15-20 minutes.
7. Remove from the oven and allow to cool for 1 minute.
8. Slide a fishslice under each ginger slice, and place on a wire tray to cool.
9. Put the cream into a basin and whip it until it is stiff. Use the cream to sandwich two ginger snap slices together.
   This pudding has to be eaten with the fingers!

Risotto

Ingredients   Serves 4
2 teacups (about 300g/12oz) rice
1 medium sized onion
1-2 teacups canned, frozen or fresh peas
1-2 teacups (about 100g/4oz) ham or cooked chicken or a mixture of both cut in 1¼cm/½in cubes
4 tablespoons sultanas
4 tablespoons peanuts
1 tablespoon soy sauce
2 tablespoons cooking oil

Tools
large frying pan and lid, saucepan, sharp knife, chopping board, tablespoon, fork, serving dish, oven gloves

Method
1. Cook the rice, *page 53.*
2. Chop the onion very finely, careful not to cut your fingers.
3. Cook the peas, *page 81.*
4. Heat the oil in a large frying pan over a low heat on the stove until a faint haze rises. This will take about 1 minute.
5. Turn down the heat and place the onion in the frying pan and stir.
6. Cover the frying pan with a lid and cook the onion for 8 minutes—do not allow it to brown so check from time to time and turn down the heat if necessary.
7. Put the rice, ham or chicken, sultanas, peanuts, peas and soy sauce in the pan and cook for 5 minutes, gently stirring all the time with a fork.
8. Put the risotto into a warm dish and serve without a vegetable.

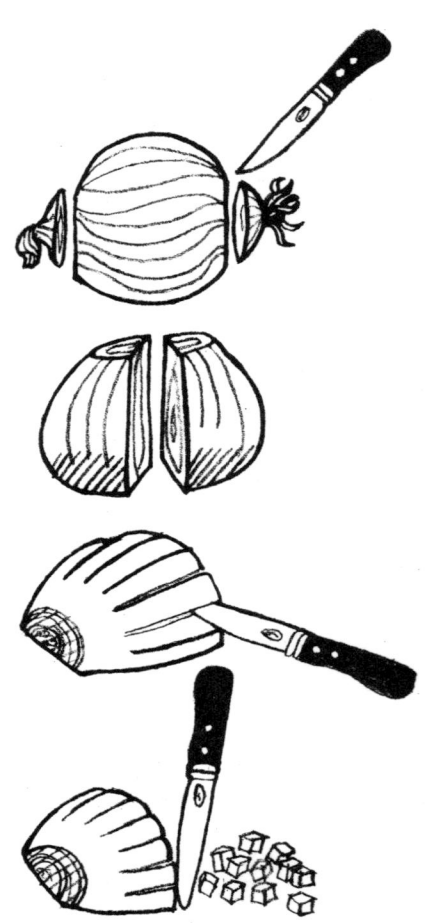

Soy sauce is used extensively in Chinese and Japanese cooking. It is one of the many by-products of the soybean which is in daily use in the East in one form or another. Soybean is one of the plants whose seedlings are eaten as bean sprouts.

Easy menus for lunch and supper

Baked Bananas

Ingredients Serves 4
4 ripe bananas
2 tablespoons golden syrup
2 tablespoons marmalade
Juice of a small orange
15g (½oz) butter

Tools
casserole and lid, or tinfoil used as a lid, tablespoon, lemon squeezer, oven gloves

Method
1. Pre-heat the oven to fairly hot (190°C, 375°F, Mark 5).
2. Squeeze the juice out of the orange.
3. Peel the bananas and place them in a casserole.
4. Pour the orange juice on to the bananas.
5. Warm the spoon under a hot water tap and spoon the golden syrup over the bananas. Next spread over the marmalade, and place the butter on top.
6. Put the lid on the casserole or cover it with tinfoil and cook on the centre shelf in the oven for 20 minutes.

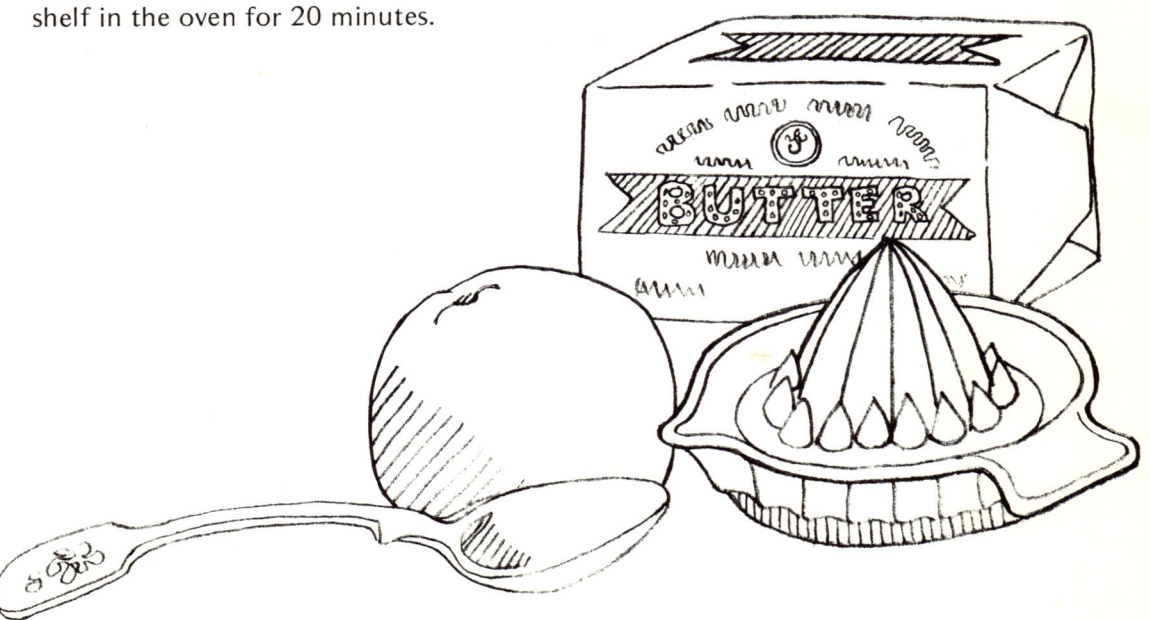

Toad-in-the-Hole

Ingredients Serves 4
8 sausages

Batter
100g (4oz) plain flour
1 egg
250ml (½ pint) milk
Pinch of salt

Tools
fork, knife, ovenproof dish, sieve, mixing basin, wooden spoon, egg beater, measuring cup, oven gloves

Method
Sausages
1. Pre-heat the oven to hot (220°C, 425°F, Mark 7).
2. Prick the sausages with a fork to prevent them bursting when they cook.
3. Place the sausages in an ovenproof dish. They should lie flat and not overlap. To make sure of crisp batter use a fairly shallow dish.
4. Put the dish on the bottom shelf of the oven and cook the sausages for 10 minutes, turn once during this time.

Batter
5. Sieve the flour into a mixing basin, add the salt.
6. Make a slight hollow in the middle with a spoon, drop in the egg.
7. Add a third of the milk and slowly stir the egg, milk and flour together.
8. Beat with a wooden spoon to get rid of any lumps.
9. Slowly add the rest of the milk, beat but be careful not to make a splash. You can use an egg beater if you like.

Toad-in-the-Hole
10. Take the casserole with sausages out of the oven.
11. Pour the batter mixture over the sausages and put the dish back in the oven on the middle shelf.
12. Cook for 30-35 minutes. Remove from the oven and serve.

Serve with gravy, *page 22* and a green vegetable or carrots.

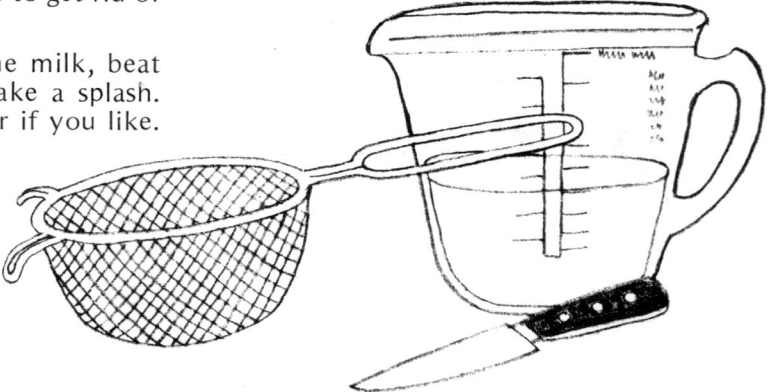

Vanilla Ice-Cream

Ingredients
125ml (¼ pint) double cream
2 egg whites
4 level tablespoons icing sugar
2-3 drops vanilla essence

Serves 3-4

Tools
egg beater, 3 basins, metal spoon, tablespoon, ice tray

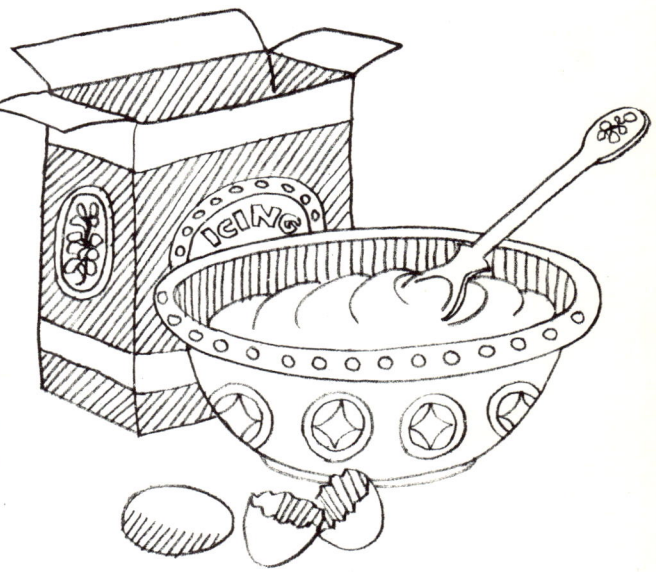

Method
1 Sift the icing sugar into a basin.
2 Separate the whites from the yolks of the eggs, *page 33*. Put the whites in a clean basin and the yolks in a covered container to keep for another recipe.
3 Put the cream into another basin and whip it with an egg beater until it thickens. It should just be able to hold its shape but not be thick enough to stand in peaks. Add the vanilla.
4 Stir the icing sugar into the cream.
5 Wash and dry the egg beater carefully. Whip the whites of egg until they are stiff.
6 Fold the egg whites into the cream mixture using a metal spoon. Pretend you are drawing a circle with the spoon and cut through to the bottom of the bowl each time.
7 Spoon the mixture into an ice tray and put it in the ice-making section of the refrigerator or in a deep freeze. It will be ready to eat in 2-3 hours.

Hot fudge sauce goes very well with ice-cream. See the recipe for Garnett fudge on *page 65*. Serve the fudge mixture hot in a bowl or spoon a little on top of each helping.

Fruit Ice-Cream
Add 1 teacupful of mashed fruit to the whipped cream at the same time as you add the icing sugar. If you make strawberry ice-cream you will need to add a few drops of red edible food colouring to the mixture.

Curried Eggs

Ingredients   Serves 4
4 eggs
150g (6oz) rice

Sauce
1 onion
1 tin tomatoes (396g/14oz)
3 tablespoons sultanas
1 eating apple
1 tablespoon flour
1-2 teaspoons curry powder
2 teacups water
25g (1oz) butter or margarine

You can make the sauce in advance as it will keep for 24 hours and can easily be heated up in a saucepan over a low heat. A selection of slices of banana, thin slices of onion and tomato, chutney and dessicated coconut in little bowls on the table will make the curried eggs all the more delicious.

Tools
chopping board, sharp knife, potato peeler, basin, frying pan and lid, tablespoon, teaspoon, teacup, 2 ovenproof dishes, saucepan, oven gloves

Method
Rice
1 Prepare the rice, *page 53.*
2 When the rice is cooked put it in a covered dish and keep warm in an oven set at its lowest temperature.

Sauce
3 Peel the onion and chop it finely.
4 Peel and core the apple and cut it into 1¼cm/½in chunks. Put it in a basin of water to help prevent it browning.
5 Melt the butter or margarine in a frying pan on a low heat. Make sure it does not burn. Turn the heat even lower if necessary.
6 Add the onion, stir thoroughly to cover it with butter, and cook very slowly with a lid on the frying pan for 8 minutes—a saucepan lid will do as it need not fit perfectly. Make sure the onion does not burn, turn down the heat if it starts to brown.
7 Stir in the flour and the curry powder.

8 Add the apple, sultanas, tomatoes and 1 teacup water. Bring to the boil by turning the heat up. Once the mixture boils turn the heat down and simmer for 15 minutes, stirring occasionally.

9 If the mixture thickens and no longer runs over the bottom of the pan, add the rest of the water.

Eggs
10 While the sauce is cooking, boil the eggs for 5 minutes *page 17*.

11 Next, the slightly difficult part: take the soft-boiled eggs out of the water using a spoon and then crack them and gently peel off the shells. Hold them under cold running water while you do this or they will burn your fingers.

Curried Eggs
12 Put the eggs in a serving dish and pour over the sauce. Eat at once otherwise the eggs will harden. Serve the rice in a separate dish.

Curry powder is not one spice but a blend of many. Some of these spices such as cloves, ginger and cinnamon are frequently used in English cooking, chilli is used more rarely but others such as coriander, turmeric, cumin, cardamon and fenugreek almost never appear in European recipes.

Miranda's Jam Pancakes

Ingredients Makes 8
50g (2oz) butter
3 tablespoons jam

Batter
100g (4oz) flour
250ml (½ pint) milk
1 egg
Pinch of salt

The batter should stand for at least 2 hours before using.

Method
Batter
1 Sieve the flour and salt together in a bowl.
2 Break the egg into a cup.
3 Make a slight hollow in the centre of the flour and drop in the egg and slowly pour in the milk.
4 Carefully stir the egg, milk and flour together to make a smooth paste without any lumps.
5 Beat well with a wooden spoon and whisk with an egg beater to remove all the lumps.
6 Cover the bowl with a saucepan lid or tinfoil and leave to stand for 2 hours.

Tools
sieve, basin, cup, wooden spoon, egg beater, lid or tinfoil, knife, tablespoon, frying pan, fishslice, meat dish or plate, measuring cup, oven gloves

Jam Pancakes
7 Set the oven to very cool (110°C, 225°F, Mark ¼).
8 Divide the butter into 8 pieces and put one of them in a frying pan.
9 Melt the piece of butter on the stove until it is hot and beginning to froth.
10 Put 2-3 tablespoons of the batter mixture in the frying pan, and spread it out as far as you can, keeping it in a circle by gently tilting the pan from side to side.
11 Spread a teaspoonful of jam over one half of the pancake. Cook for 2-3 minutes then fold.
12 Remove carefully from the pan with a fishslice, place on a dish, sprinkle with sugar and keep warm in the oven while you cook the rest of the pancakes.

Pancakes don't keep hot very well so eat them as soon as you can. For traditional pancakes, eaten with sugar and a squeeze of lemon, cook the pancakes for 1½ minutes on each side. Turn them over with a fishslice, if the pancakes are as thin as they should be this is not particularly easy to do!

Easy menus for lunch and supper

Kedgeree

Ingredients Serves 4
200g (8oz) smoked cod
200g (8oz) fresh cod
2 hard-boiled eggs, *page 55*
100g (4oz) butter
200g (8oz) round or pudding rice
Salt and pepper

Tools
sieve, basin, saucepan, frying pan, wooden spoon, fishslice, teaspoon, chopping board, knife, oven gloves

Method
1. Cook the rice *page 53*.
2. While the rice is cooking put enough water in a frying pan to cover the fish. Bring the water to the boil.
3. Put both kinds of fish in the water and cook them slowly. The water should simmer for 10 minutes.
4. Remove the pan from the heat and lift the fish out of the water with a fishslice.
5. Allow the fish to cool a little, but while it is still warm remove all the bones and the skin and break it up into small pieces.
6. Take the shells off the hard-boiled eggs, put them on a chopping board and cut into small pieces with a knife.
7. Melt the butter in a saucepan over a low heat.
8. Add the fish and rice. Turn the heat very low and stir well. Taste, and add salt and pepper. Next gently stir in the chopped egg.
9. Remove the pan from the stove, put the kedgeree in a dish and keep it hot in an oven set as low as it will go.

Serve bread and butter with kedgeree. This is a dish which is generally eaten without a vegetable. Incidentally, kedgeree reheats easily. Put it in a basin, cover the top tightly with tinfoil and sit the basin over a saucepan containing simmering water. Make sure the water does not boil otherwise the pan will quickly become dry and burn! This is a good, safe way to heat up almost any dish, including vegetables.

Macaroni Cheese

Ingredients
150g (6oz) macaroni
1½ litres (2½ pints) water
¼ teaspoon salt

Sauce
375ml (¾ pint) milk
2½ tablespoons flour
75g (3oz) Cheddar cheese
25g (1oz) butter or margarine
Pepper and ¼ teaspoon salt

Topping
3 tablespoons dried breadcrumbs
25g (1oz) grated Cheddar cheese
25g (1oz) butter or margarine

Serves 4

Tools
grater, measuring cup, fork, 2 saucepans, tablespoon, sieve, teaspoon, ovenproof dish, small basin, knife, oven gloves

Method
Macaroni

1. Put the water in a saucepan with the salt and bring it to the boil on the stove.

2. While the water is coming to the boil break the macaroni into lengths of about 5cm/2in.

3. Put the macaroni into the boiling water. When the water starts bubbling rapidly, turn down the heat and cook it gently for about 15-20 minutes depending on its thickness. Test by lifting a piece out of the water. If it is cooked you can cut it easily with the edge of a fork.

4. Remove the pan from the stove and pour the macaroni into a sieve to drain it. Once it has drained put it in an ovenproof dish.

5. While the macaroni is cooking make the sauce.

Easy menus for lunch and supper

Sauce

6 First grate the cheese.

7 Melt the butter or margarine over a low heat in a saucepan on the stove.

8 Remove the saucepan from the stove and slowly stir in the flour. Add the salt and two shakes of pepper.

9 Put the saucepan back on the heat and cook this mixture, which is called a 'roux', until it bubbles and begins to turn straw-coloured.

10 Take the pan off the stove once more and with great care very slowly stir in the milk, making sure that there are no lumps.

11 Put the saucepan back on the stove again and stir the mixture all the time until it thickens.

12 Add the grated cheese to the sauce and cook it for 1-2 minutes.

13 Pour the sauce over the macaroni.

Topping

14 Mix the cheese and the breadcrumbs together and sprinkle these evenly over the macaroni cheese.

15 Cut the butter into about 8 pieces and dot these over the breadcrumbs and cheese mixture.

16 Put the dish under the grill and cook until the surface looks golden brown. This will take 3-4 minutes.

Serve with a green salad, *page 83* or with a hot vegetable. Carrots or green beans would make a good choice, *pages 81, 82.*

Chocolate Queens Pudding

Ingredients Serves 4
250ml (½ pint) milk
2 egg yolks
75g (3oz) fresh breadcrumbs
   (3-4 slices bread)*
2 tablespoons cocoa
2 tablespoons sugar
2 tablespoons apricot or
   raspberry jam

Meringue
2 egg whites
3 tablespoons castor sugar

* Fresh breadcrumbs can be made by either rubbing stale, crustless bread against a cheese grater .or by breaking fresh or stale bread up in an electric blender. Only blend 1 slice of crustless bread at a time.

Tools
grater, blender, 2 basins, egg beater, 2 tablespoons, fork, small ovenproof dish, measuring cup, oven gloves

Method
Chocolate Pudding

1. Separate the whites from the yolks of the eggs and put them in two separate basins, *page 33*.

2. Lightly beat the yolks with a fork and add the cocoa, sugar and milk. Stir in the breadcrumbs.

3. Put the breadcrumb mixture into an ovenproof dish and place in a 'moderate' oven (180°C, 350°F, Mark 4). Cook for 25 minutes until the mixture appears firm.

4. Take the pudding out of the oven and cover the surface with jam. Turn the oven down to cool (150°C, 300°F, Mark 2).

5. Whip the whites of egg for the meringue and when they are stiff and able to stand in peaks, slowly fold in the sugar with a spoon, a tablespoon at a time.

6. Pile the meringue mixture on top of the pudding and return the dish to the oven. Cook for another 20 minutes in the 'cool' oven to crisp the meringue.

Saucy Omelette

Ingredients   Serves 4
6 eggs
25g (1oz) butter
Salt and pepper

Sauce
(or use packet of cheese sauce mix)
250ml (½ pint) milk
100g (4oz) grated cheese
1½ tablespoons flour
25g (1oz) butter or margarine
1 tablespoon chopped parsley
Salt and pepper

Tools
frying pan (25cm/10in diameter), saucepan, tablespoon, wooden spoon, fork, grater, chopping board, knife, fishslice, basin, measuring cup, oven gloves

Method
Sauce
1. Chop the parsley and grate the cheese.
2. Then melt the butter or margarine in a saucepan over a low heat.
3. Take it off the stove and slowly stir in the flour and add the salt and 2 shakes of pepper.
4. Put the saucepan back on the heat and cook this mixture, which is called a 'roux' until it bubbles and begins to change colour slightly.
5. Take the pan off the stove once more and very slowly stir in the milk, making sure that there are no lumps.
6. Put the saucepan back on the stove again and stir the mixture without stopping until it thickens. (If the worst happens and the sauce becomes lumpy you can put it through a sieve. This doesn't entirely save the sauce, but it helps!).
7. Keep 2 tablespoons of cheese on one side and add the rest to the sauce. Cook for 1-2 minutes. Taste and add salt and pepper.
8. Remove the pan from the heat and add the parsley.

Omelette

9. Break the eggs into a basin.
10. Add salt and pepper and 2 tablespoons of water to the eggs and beat them lightly with a fork.
11. Melt the butter in a frying pan until it is hot and foaming.
12. Pour the egg mixture into the frying pan; stir once or twice with the flat of the fork.
13. As the omelette firms, carefully lift the sides with a fishslice to allow the uncooked egg to run to the bottom. Shake the pan gently from side to side to keep the omelette from sticking.
14. When the omelette is firm underneath but just soft on top cover the surface evenly with the sauce.
15. Sprinkle the top evenly with the remaining 2 tablespoonfuls of grated cheese.
16. Put the omelette under the grill and cook until the surface of the sauce is light brown. Be very careful that the handle of the frying pan is not grilled, too!
17. Divide in four and serve directly on to hot plates.

A side dish of winter or summer salad goes well with saucy omelette, *pages 86, 83.*

Cherry Flan

Ingredients Serves 4

Pastry flan case
150g (6oz) plain flour
35g (1½oz) butter or margarine
35g (1½oz) lard
Pinch of salt
About 2 tablespoons water
If you are using frozen pastry turn to the flan case instructions below

Filling
1 tin red cherries (425g/15oz)
1 tablespoon arrowroot or cornflour
1 tablespoon lemon juice
A few drops edible red food colouring

Tools
tablespoon, 2 basins, knife, rolling pin, pastry board, sieve, flan tin (17½cm/7in diameter), tin-opener, tinfoil, buttered paper, saucepan, oven gloves

Method
Pastry

1. Sieve the flour and salt into a mixing basin.
2. Cut the fat into small pieces.
3. Mix by running the flour and fat between your fingers and thumbs. Try not to get any flour on the palms of your hands. Continue until the mixture looks like fine breadcrumbs.
4. Mix to a stiff dough with water, a tablespoonful at a time, and use your hands to draw the mixture into a ball of dough which holds together. If the mixture tries to break apart, add a little more water.
5. Keep the dough in a cool place for 30 minutes before using it.
6. Pre-heat the oven to fairly hot (200°C, 400°F, Mark 6).

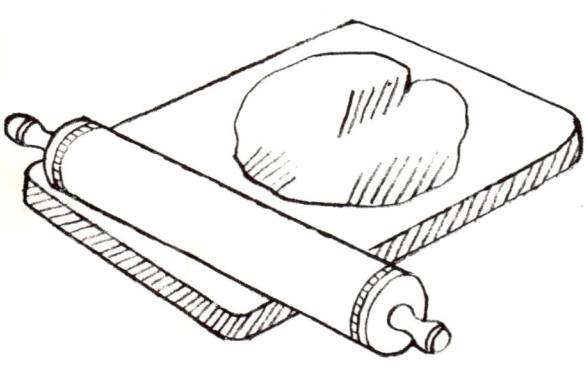

Flan case

7 Sprinkle some flour on a pastry board and flatten out the pastry dough to a neat, round shape with your knuckles.

8 Roll it out with a rolling pin to a thickness of about ½cm/¼in. Try to keep the pastry round to fit the flan tin.

9 Cut a piece of tinfoil to line the bottom of the flan tin, and also cut strips about 6cm/2½in wide to cover the edges. Put the tinfoil on one side and grease the tin with a piece of buttered paper.

10 Lay the pastry over the flan tin and gently ease it at the edges so that it lines the side of the tin. Cut round the edge to trim the pastry.

11 Cover the pastry with the tinfoil. Press it firmly down on the bottom to stop the pastry rising as it cooks.

12 Put on the middle shelf in the oven and cook for 30 minutes. Take the flan out of the oven and remove the tinfoil.

The Filling

13 Open the tin of cherries, remove the stones and strain the juice into a basin through a sieve.

14 Put the arrowroot or cornflour in a saucepan and stir in the cherry juice a little at a time. Add the lemon juice.

15 Heat the mixture on the stove and stir until the arrowroot thickens. Cook for 1 minute stirring all the time.

16 Remove the saucepan from the heat. Add the red colouring.

17 Line the flan case with the cherries.

18 Cool the arrowroot mixture to blood temperature and spoon over the cherries.

19 Leave to set.

Cherry flan can be eaten on its own but it is particularly good with whipped cream.

Charlotte's Fruit Milk Jelly

Ingredients Serves 4
1 tin fruit (439g/15½oz)
1 orange jelly
250ml (½ pint) milk
250ml (½ pint) water and
  fruit juice

Tools
saucepan, sieve, basin, tin-opener, spoon, jelly mould, measuring cup, oven gloves

This jelly is made in two parts. Although the action time is short the waiting between the two parts requires a little patience. Blood-temperature is referred to in this recipe and means a temperature which feels neither hot nor cold when you put your finger in it; in other words the temperature is the same as that of your blood.

Method
Milk Jelly
1. Rinse the jelly mould out in cold water.
2. Separate the orange jelly squares.
3. Heat the milk in a saucepan. As soon as it boils quickly remove it from the stove. Count up to 60 and then put half the orange jelly squares in the milk. Stir to help the jelly dissolve.
4. Pour the milk jelly into the mould and leave in a cool place. Once it has cooled to blood temperature you can put it in a refrigerator. It will take about 2 hours to set.

Fruit Jelly
5. Open the tin of fruit and drain the juice into a measuring cup with the help of a sieve. Make the juice up to 250ml/½ pint by adding water. Put the fruit in a basin.
6. When the milk jelly has almost set firm pour the fruit juice and water mixture into a saucepan. Put it on the heat and bring the juice to the boil. Remove the saucepan from the stove and again count up to 60 before stirring in the remaining jelly squares. Add the fruit.
7. Once the fruit jelly has cooled to blood temperature spoon it on to the set milk jelly. Leave to get firm in a refrigerator, preferably over night.
8. When the fruit milk jelly is firm give the mould a good shake and turn it out on to a plate.

Easy menus for lunch and supper

Rice

Ingredients
150g (6oz) patna rice
1 litre (1¾ pints) water
¼ teaspoon salt

Serves 4

Tools
basin, sieve, saucepan, fork, oven gloves

Method
1. Wash the rice in a basin. Change the water several times using a sieve, if necessary. Finally pour the rice into a sieve to drain.
2. Put the water in a saucepan and bring it to the boil. When it is fast-boiling add the rice and salt. Adding the rice will cool the water. Once it starts to boil fast again turn the heat down a little so that the water only bubbles gently.
3. At the end of the cooking time the rice should be firm. Start testing after 12 minutes by removing a grain with a fork. Cool it before eating it. It should not take more than 15 minutes to cook so be careful about the timing as rice becomes mushy with too much cooking.
4. Once the rice has cooled drain it in a sieve. Keep warm in an ovenproof dish in a very cool oven (110°C, 225°F, Mark ¼). Turn with a fork a few times.

Casual Snacks for Hungry Friends

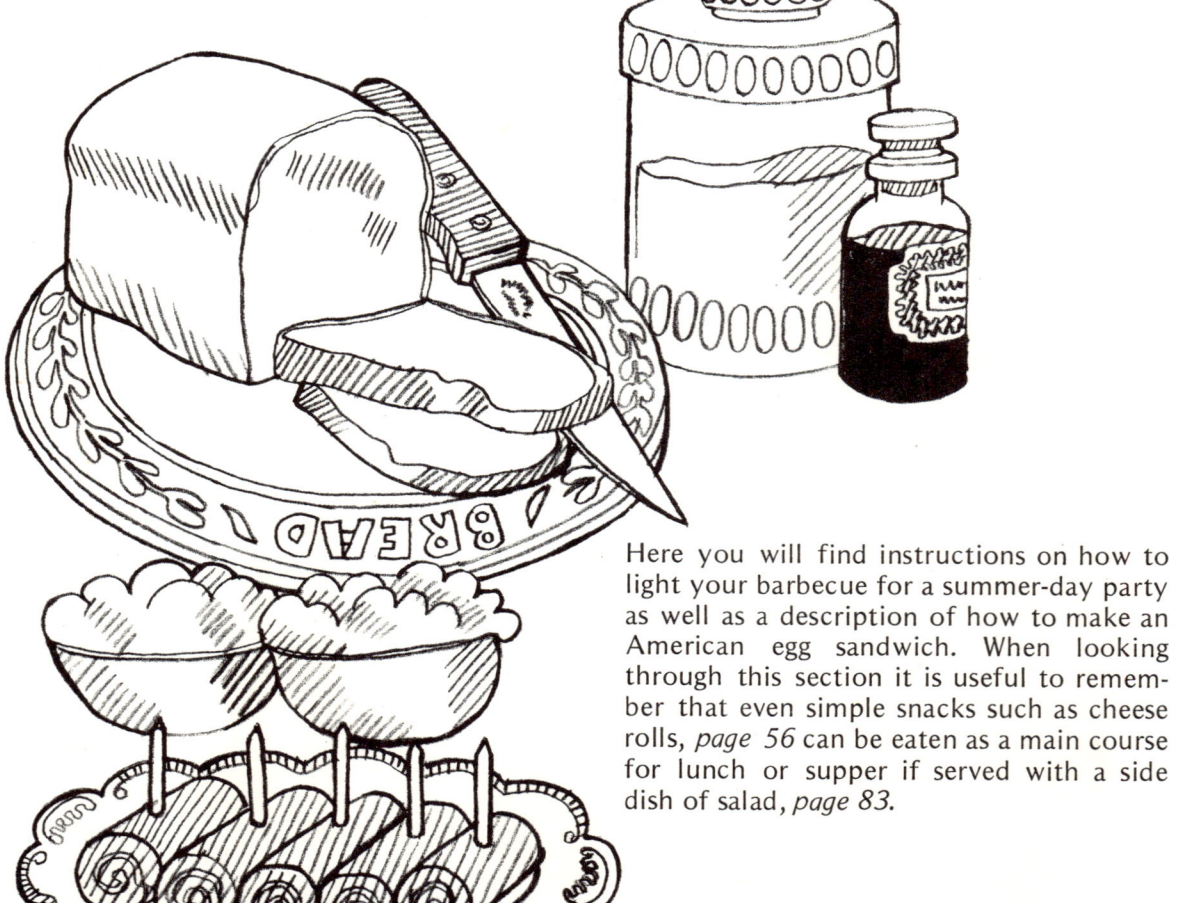

Here you will find instructions on how to light your barbecue for a summer-day party as well as a description of how to make an American egg sandwich. When looking through this section it is useful to remember that even simple snacks such as cheese rolls, *page 56* can be eaten as a main course for lunch or supper if served with a side dish of salad, *page 83*.

American Egg Sandwiches

Ingredients
Allow the following per person:
2 hard-boiled eggs
2 slices bread
2 tablespoons egg mayonnaise or
 1 tablespoon salad cream
1 teaspoon onion or spring onion
1 lettuce leaf (not essential)
15g (½oz) butter
Pepper and salt

Tools
saucepan, fork, basin, knife, tablespoon, chopping board

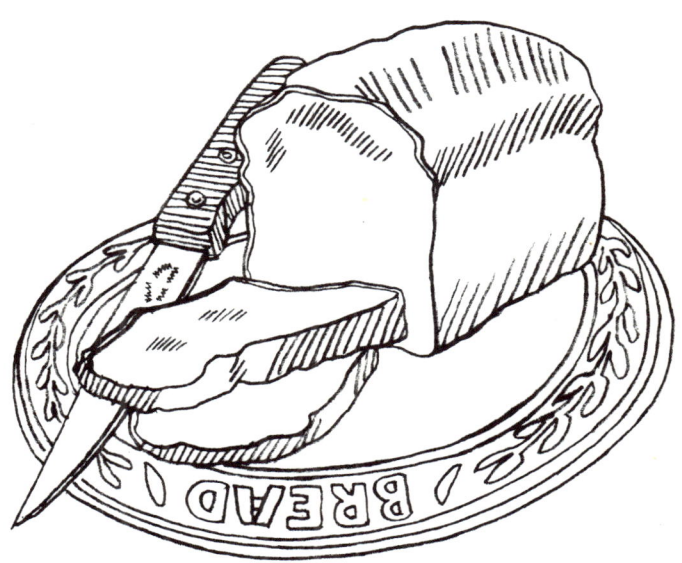

Method
1 Hard-boil the eggs by cooking them in boiling water for 10 minutes. Once the eggs are cooked pour off the boiling water and immediately replace it with cold.
2 Chop the onion or spring onion into very small pieces.
3 Remove the shells from the eggs and put the eggs in a basin. Cut them up so that they get cold quickly.
4 Once the egg has cooled add the mayonnaise or salad cream, onion, salt and pepper and mash the mixture up thoroughly with a fork. Taste, and add more salt and pepper if necessary.
5 Put the bread under the grill and toast it on one side only. Watch carefully so that it does not burn.
6 Remove the bread from the grill and butter the untoasted side.
7 Take one of the two slices and place it on a board with the buttered side facing upwards. Spoon on the egg mixture and smooth it out evenly over the bread with a knife. Place the lettuce leaf on top. Cover with the other slice of bread, the buttered side facing downwards.

It is a good idea to eat this kind of sandwich with a knife and fork!

Casual snacks for hungry friends

Rupert's Cheese Rolls

Ingredients
8 slices of bread
4 slices of processed cheese
25g (1oz) butter
Mustard

Makes 8

Tools
chopping board, knife, rolling pin, cocktail sticks, baking tray, oven gloves

Method
1 Pre-heat the oven to moderate (180°C, 350°F, Mark 4).
2 Cut the crusts off the bread.
3 Flatten the slices of bread with a rolling pin. This will help it roll up.
4 Cut the slices of processed cheese in half.
5 Butter the bread, lay a piece of processed cheese across it and spread over a little mustard.
6 Roll the bread and cheese up and secure the rolls at each end with a cocktail stick or toothpick.
7 Place the rolls on a baking tray and cook on the middle shelf of the oven for about 20 minutes.
8 Serve hot.

Casual snacks for hungry friends

Egg Nests

Ingredients Serves 4
4 bread rolls
4 eggs
4 tablespoons grated Cheddar cheese
25g (1oz) butter
Salt and pepper

Tools
knife, spoon, basin, egg beater, tablespoon, baking tray, oven gloves

Method

1. Pre-heat the oven to fairly hot (190°C, 375°F, Mark 5).
2. Cut the rolls in half and scoop out enough bread to leave only a thin shell. Store the scooped-out bread in a plastic bag to use for meat loaf or some other dish needing breadcrumbs.
3. Divide the butter and the grated cheese between the four bread roll baskets. Start with the butter, place the cheese on top and smooth with a spoon.
4. Sprinkle a little pepper and a pinch of salt inside each basket.
5. Separate the whites from the yolks of egg. Put the whites together in a basin and a yolk in each basket; take great care not to break the yolks while you are doing this.
6. Whip the egg whites until they are stiff and divide into four. Place a mound of egg white on each egg yolk.
7. Place the egg basket on a baking tray and cook on the middle shelf of the oven for 10 minutes. The timing is important as the egg yolks will harden if they are cooked for too long.

Barbecued Food

Sprinkle lighter fuel over the charcoal briquets and leave it to soak in for a little while. Persuade an adult to light the charcoal as this can be a dangerous and frustrating business. Start lighting the charcoal about ¾ hour before you want to cook. The timing does depend a little on the kind of grill you have, though it is better to be ready early and have to add more briquets than keep hungry people waiting for hours! Add more lighter fuel if you have difficulty getting the charcoal to burn. The charcoal is ready to use for cooking when it is grey all over.

Barbecued Frankfurters

Ingredients
Allow 2 frankfurters and
  2 frankfurter rolls per person

Tools
knife, long-handled fork,
fishslice or palette knife,
spoon, oven gloves

Method
1. Put the frankfurters on the grill over the charcoal.
2. Cook for about 6 minutes until they look cooked but not burnt; turn them over sometimes. It is difficult to give exact timing as this depends on the amount of heat coming from the charcoal fire.
3. Cut open the rolls and put a frankfurter in each. You can add mustard, chutney or tomato sauce, too, if you like. There are also recipes on *page 60* for two special barbeque sauces which you may like to try.

If you want to make the frankfurters look more interesting slice each end down about 2½cm/1in in the shape of a cross; this will make the ends curl up while they are cooking. Frankfurters also taste good sliced through the middle from one end to the other and grilled in two halves.

Barbecued Hamburgers*

Ingredients
Allow 100g (4oz) best minced beef per person and 1 hamburger bun.
For 4 people or 2 hungry ones!
400g (16oz) minced beef
1 tablespoon mixed herbs
1 tablespoon grated or finely
  chopped onion
Pepper and ¼ teaspoon salt

Tools
grater of knife, chopping board, basin, tablespoon, teaspoon, long-handled fishslice or palette knife, oven gloves

Method
1. Put the meat, herbs, onion, salt and pepper together in a basin and mix together thoroughly with a spoon.
2. Take the mixture out of the bowl and form into four hamburgers. (If you are cooking for two hungry people who also like their hamburgers very pink in the middle make 2 thick hamburgers instead of 4 thin ones.)
3. Cook the hamburgers on the grill over the charcoal for 5-8 minutes on each side. It is difficult to be exact about timing as this depends on the heat coming from your grill.
4. Cut open the hamburger rolls and put the cooked hamburgers inside. You can also add a thin slice of uncooked onion and some chutney or tomato sauce or one of the two barbecue sauces which follow this recipe.

* The frankfurters and hamburgers can of course be grilled under a gas or electric grill if you do not have a charcoal grill or if it is raining!

Quick Barbecue Sauces

Hot Sauce

Ingredients
3 tablespoons tomato ketchup
1 teaspoon Worcestershire sauce
¼ teaspoon ready-made English mustard
¼ teaspoon celery salt or salt

Tools
small bowl, tablespoon, teaspoon

Method
Put all the above ingredients in a bowl and mix thoroughly with a spoon. This makes a very hot sauce so leave out the mustard if you prefer something cooler.

Sweet Sauce

Ingredients
3 tablespoons tomato ketchup
1 teaspoon Worcestershire sauce
1 teaspoon maple or golden syrup
¼ teaspoon mustard

Tools
small bowl, tablespoon, teaspoon

Method
Put all the ingredients together in a bowl and mix well with a spoon. This sauce is fairly hot, too, but you can always use less than a ¼ teaspoon of mustard if you prefer it cooler.

For a change try these sauces with fish fingers.

Casual snacks for hungry friends

Caramel Toast

Ingredients Serves 4
4 slices bread
6 tablespoons demerara sugar
25g (1oz) butter

Tools
bread knife, board,
tablespoon, oven gloves

Method

1. Put the bread under the grill and toast on one side only. Watch carefully to see that it does not burn.

2. Remove the toast from the grill and spread the untoasted side with butter. Next spread the sugar over, making sure that there is only a thin coating of sugar round the edge of each slice otherwise it will melt and slide off when you put the slices under the grill!

3. Put the sugar-coated slices of bread under the heat and cook until the sugar melts and bubbles. When you can smell caramel the toast is ready. Watch carefully while the sugar is heating to make sure that it does not burn, turning down the heat if necessary.

4. Cool a little before eating otherwise you will burn your tongue!

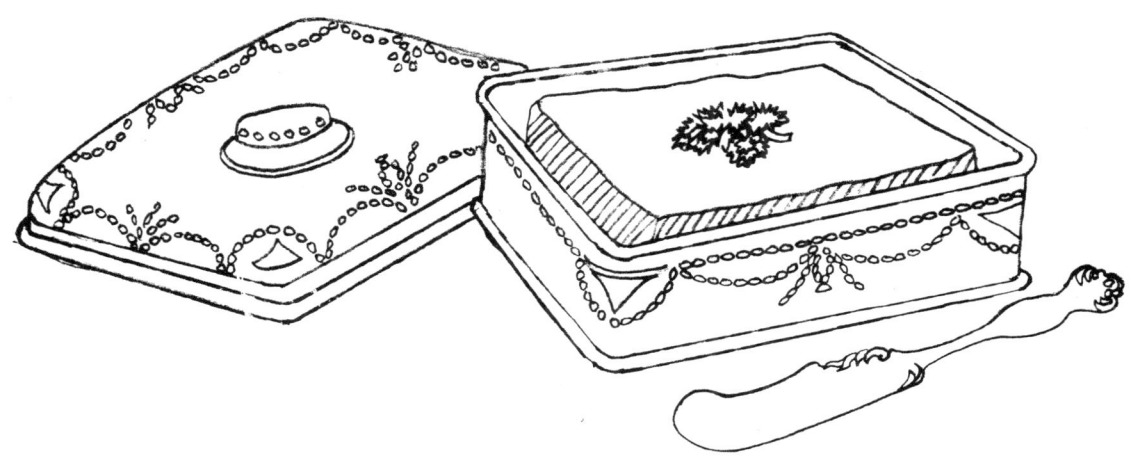

French Toast

Ingredients
2 slices thick bread cut from a large loaf
1 egg
3 tablespoons milk
Pinch of salt
1 teaspoon sugar
25g (1oz) butter

Serves 4

Tools
bread knife, chopping board, soup bowl or shallow dish, fork, frying pan, saucepan, tablespoon, oven gloves

Method
1. Break the egg into a soup bowl or shallow dish.
2. Beat the egg lightly with a fork and add the milk, sugar and salt.
3. Cut the crusts off the bread, and then cut each slice in two.
4. Heat the butter in a frying pan on the stove until it starts to froth and bubble. Do not let it turn brown and burn.
5. Meanwhile soak the bread in the egg mixture.
6. Put the soaked bread into the frying pan and cook for about 4 minutes on each side until golden brown. It is important when frying to watch carefully and be ready quickly to turn the heat up or down.

French toast is delicious eaten with golden syrup. Try American style eating, French toast with syrup and sausages!

Casual snacks for hungry friends

Cinnamon Toast

Ingredients
4 slices of bread
1 teaspoon ground cinnamon
1 tablespoon sugar
50g (2oz) butter

Serves 4

Tools
bread knife, board, teaspoon, tablespoon, saucepan, oven gloves

Method
1. Toast the bread *page 17*.
2. Melt the butter in a saucepan on the stove.
3. Once the butter has melted add the cinnamon and sugar. Cook for 1 minute and then spoon over the toast. Serve immediately.

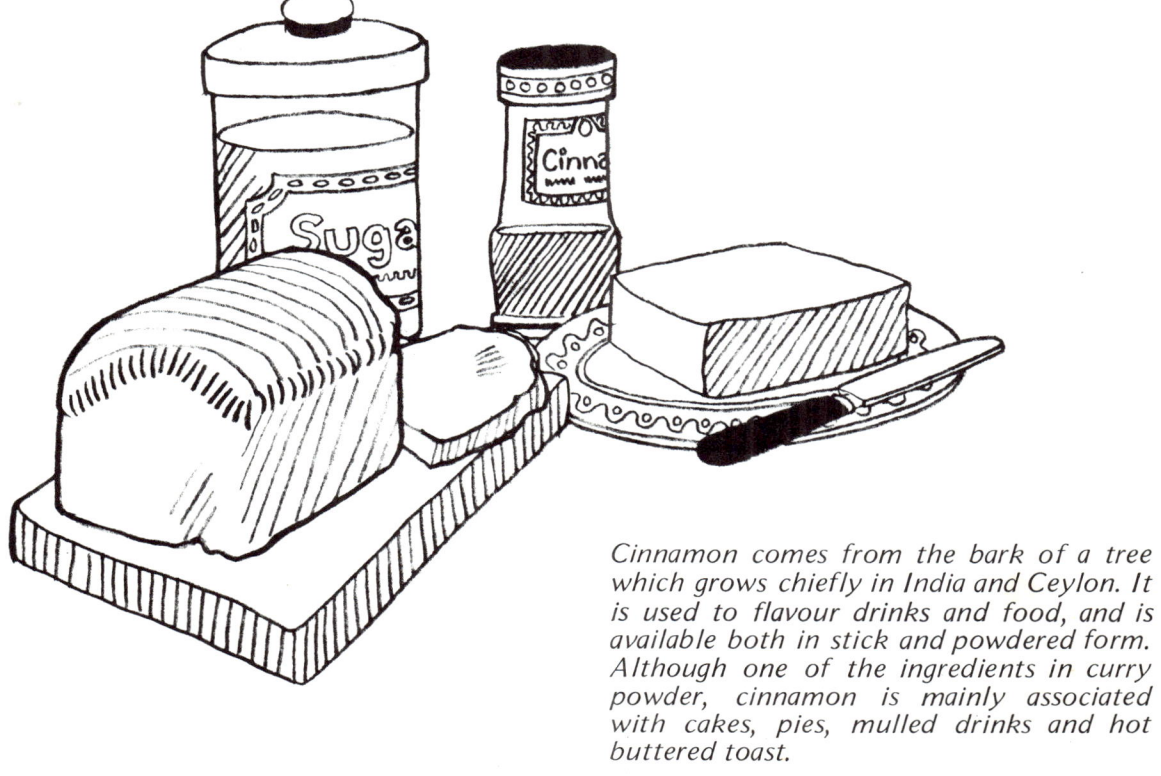

Cinnamon comes from the bark of a tree which grows chiefly in India and Ceylon. It is used to flavour drinks and food, and is available both in stick and powdered form. Although one of the ingredients in curry powder, cinnamon is mainly associated with cakes, pies, mulled drinks and hot buttered toast.

Sweets and Biscuits to Eat or Give Away

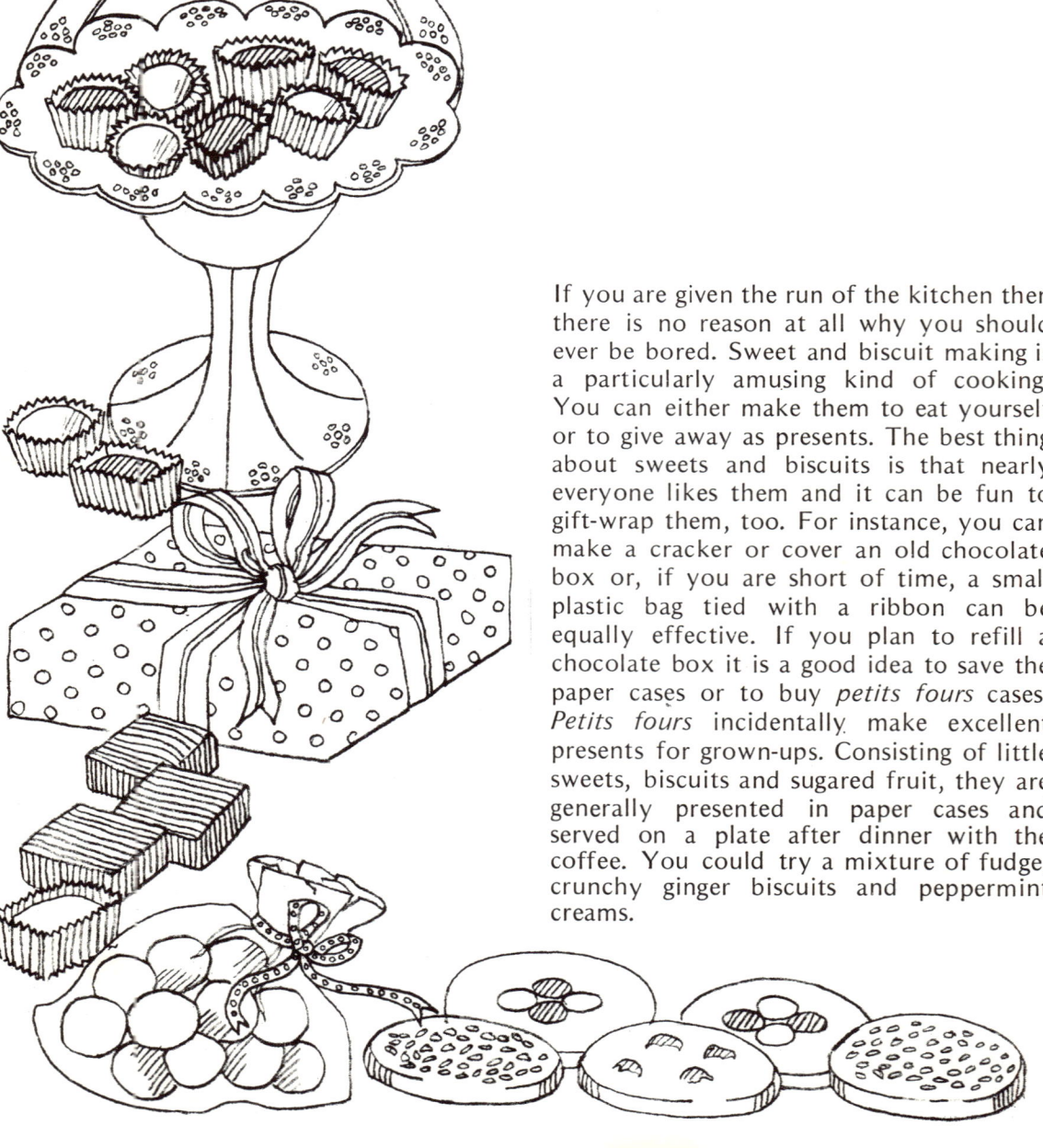

If you are given the run of the kitchen then there is no reason at all why you should ever be bored. Sweet and biscuit making is a particularly amusing kind of cooking. You can either make them to eat yourself or to give away as presents. The best thing about sweets and biscuits is that nearly everyone likes them and it can be fun to gift-wrap them, too. For instance, you can make a cracker or cover an old chocolate box or, if you are short of time, a small plastic bag tied with a ribbon can be equally effective. If you plan to refill a chocolate box it is a good idea to save the paper cases or to buy *petits fours* cases. *Petits fours* incidentally make excellent presents for grown-ups. Consisting of little sweets, biscuits and sugared fruit, they are generally presented in paper cases and served on a plate after dinner with the coffee. You could try a mixture of fudge, crunchy ginger biscuits and peppermint creams.

Sweets and biscuits to eat or give away

Garnett Fudge

Ingredients
400g (1lb) sugar
50g (2oz) butter
125ml (¼ pint) sweetened condensed milk
125ml (¼ pint) milk
3 tablespoons cocoa or 1½ tablespoons coffee essence

Tools
saucepan, tablespoon, knife, fork, flan tin (17½cm/7in diameter) or small rectangular tin, buttered paper, oven gloves

Method
1 Grease the flan tin with a piece of buttered paper.
2 Put the sugar, butter, condensed milk, milk and cocoa or coffee essence together in a saucepan.
3 Put the saucepan on the stove over a low heat and bring to the boil.
4 Turn the heat down even lower and let the mixture bubble gently for 40 minutes. Stir every few minutes otherwise the fudge mixture will stick to the bottom of the pan and burn.
5 Remove the pan from the stove and beat the mixture with a fork until it thickens.
6 Pour the fudge into the greased tray, mark the fudge in inch squares with a knife as soon as it is firm enough to hold the marking, and leave to set.

Toffee Apples

Ingredients
150g (6oz) white sugar
1½ tablespoons water
4 eating apples
4 sticks the thickness of
  pencils or chopsticks

Tools
saucepan, tablespoon, jam jar, oven gloves

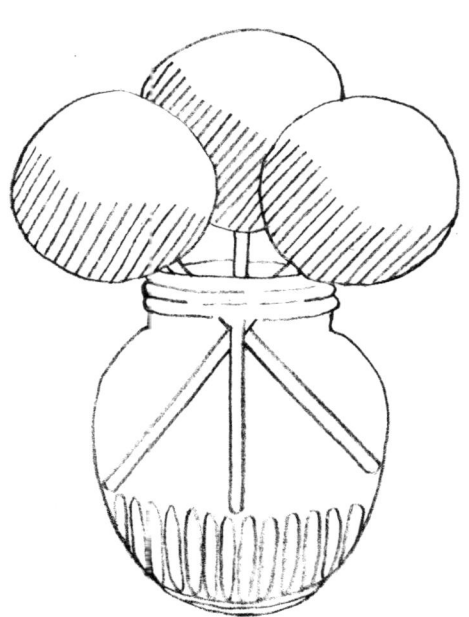

Method
1. Push the sticks firmly into the cores of the apples.
2. Put the sugar and water in a saucepan and put it on the stove.
3. The sugar will melt and turn golden brown after a few minutes. Once the sugar starts to turn brown, stir it so that the sugar is coloured evenly all over. Remove from the stove before it burns.
4. Roll the apples in the syrup mixture, one at a time.
5. Stand the toffee apples stick end down in a jam jar, balancing them carefully, otherwise the jar will fall over! Spoon over the remaining syrup before it hardens in the bottom of the pan.

Peppermint Creams

Ingredients
400g (1lb) icing sugar
1 large egg white
½ teaspoon peppermint essence
1 tablespoon water
For coffee creams replace the water and peppermint essence with 1 tablespoon coffee essence.

Tools
sieve, basin, rolling pin, egg beater, chopping board, teaspoon, tablespoon, knife or round cutter (diameter about 2½cm/1in)

Method
1. Sieve the icing sugar. If the lumps of icing sugar are very hard put them in a plastic bag and crush them with a rolling pin before sieving.
2. Separate the white from the yolk of the egg, *page 33*. Put the yolk in a small covered container and keep for use in something else.
3. Whip the white of egg with an egg beater until it is stiff.
4. Stir the egg white into the icing sugar a spoonful at a time. Add the peppermint essence and the water.
5. Gather the mixture together by squeezing it with your hands. This will be quite difficult but try not to add any more water. The mixture should end by looking liked a packed snowball.
6. Put the mixture on a pastry board and flatten it with a rolling pin to a thickness of about 1cm/½in. If you have not got a cutter divide it into small triangles with a knife.
7. Leave to dry for 24 hours—try not to have too many tastes before the peppermint creams are ready!

Vanilla Biscuits

Ingredients — Makes about 25
200g (8oz) flour
100g (4oz) butter or margarine
100g (4oz) sugar
1 teaspoon baking powder
1 egg yolk
2-3 tablespoons milk
Few drops vanilla essence
Crystallized cherries or flaked almonds, though these are not essential

Tools
mixing basin, basin, fork, wooden spoon, cup, teaspoon, sieve, rolling pin, pastry board, pastry cutter (5½cm/2¼in across), baking trays, cake rack, fishslice, buttered paper, oven gloves

Method

1. Pre-heat the oven to moderate (180°C, 350°F, Mark 4).
2. Put the sugar, margarine or butter, cut in small pieces, in a mixing basin.
3. Stir and then beat with a fork. This is called creaming. When the mixture is ready it looks like very thick cream.
4. Separate the white from the yolk of egg, *page 33*. Put the white in a covered container to use later for meringues, ice-cream or peppermint creams. Put the yolk in a cup and beat it with a fork.
5. Sieve the flour into a basin and add the baking powder.
6. Slowly beat the flour into the butter and sugar mixture using a wooden spoon.
7. Add the egg yolk a spoonful at a time and beat well. Add the milk and the drops of vanilla.
8. Knead the mixture with your knuckles and gather it together to form a ball. If it doesn't hold together add a little milk or water.
9. Put some flour on a pastry board. Place the biscuit mixture on the board and divide it in two.
10. Grease the baking tin with buttered paper.
11. Dust the rolling pin with flour and roll out the biscuit mixture until it is ¼cm/⅛in thick. Cut into biscuits with a pastry cutter. At this stage the biscuits can be decorated with small pieces of crystallized cherry or one or two flaked almonds.
12. Place the biscuits on the baking trays; the mixture does not spread very much while cooking so you need not leave more that about 2cm/1in between each biscuit. You will probably have to cook these biscuits in two batches.
13. Put the trays on the centre shelves of the oven and cook for about 13 minutes until they are just beginning to change colour.
14. Take the biscuits out of the oven and lift them from the trays using a fish-slice. Put the biscuits on a cake rack and leave to get cold.

Once they are cold these biscuits can be decorated with water icing and sprinkled with hundreds-and-thousands, silver balls or Smarties, water icing *page 74*. For presents, pack the biscuits in layers in an empty chocolate box covered with pretty paper. Put a sheet of greaseproof paper between each layer of biscuits. If you are in a hurry put the biscuits in small plastic bags and then tie them up with gay ribbon bows.

Sweets and biscuits to eat or give away

Chocolate Krispies

Ingredients   Makes about 20
50g (2oz) plain chocolate
2 tablespoons golden syrup
1 tablespoon cocoa
25g (1oz) butter
50g (2oz) Rice Krispies

Tools
saucepan, tablespoon, wooden spoon, knife, scissors, greaseproof paper, oven gloves

Method
1. Break the chocolate in small pieces.
2. Put the chocolate, butter, golden syrup and cocoa in a saucepan. You will find it easier to measure the golden syrup if you warm the spoon first.
3. Put the saucepan on the stove over a low heat. Stir the mixture with a spoon to blend the chocolate, butter, syrup and cocoa well together until they have completely melted.
4. Remove the saucepan from the stove and stir in the Rice Krispies.
5. The Krispie mixture can then either be placed in mounds on buttered greaseproof paper or shaped into boats. Put in a refrigerator to harden and store in a cool place.

Rice Krispie Boats

Ingredients   Makes about 14-16
Chocolate Krispie mixture
4 sheets rice paper 28cm/11in by 17½cm/7in
Cocktail sticks

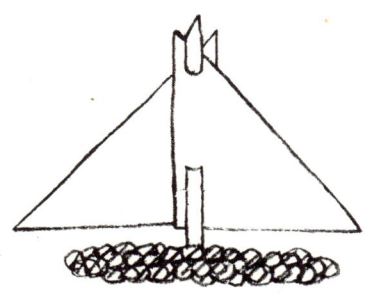

Method
1. Shape the Rice Krispie mixture into a boat with the help of a knife. It should measure about 10cm/4in long.
2. Make sails by cutting the rice paper in 9cm/3½in squares. Then cut a square diagonally across to make 2 sails.
3. Lay the sails side by side and overlap them 1cm/½in. Secure down the centre with a cocktail stick.
4. When the Krispie mixture has set cut round the rice paper with a knife, and stick the cocktail stick into the middle of the Krispie boat.

You can of course eat rice paper!

Crunchy Ginger Biscuits

Ingredients Makes about 25
125g (5oz) flour
½ teaspoon bicarbonate of soda
100g (4oz) butter
100g (4oz) demerara sugar
2 teaspoons powdered ginger
1 egg

Tools
mixing basin, basin, sieve, teaspoon, fork, wooden spoon, baking trays, teaspoon, fishslice, cake rack, buttered paper, oven gloves

Method
1. Pre-heat the oven to fairly hot (180°C, 375°F, Mark 5).
2. Put the butter and sugar together in a mixing basin and beat with a fork until it begins to look like very thick cream. If the butter is soft this will only take 2-3 minutes.
3. Break the egg into the bowl with the sugar and butter, add the ginger and beat again.
4. Sieve the flour into a basin and add the bicarbonate of soda.
5. Add the flour slowly to the sugar and butter mixture and beat, preferably with a wooden spoon.
6. Grease the baking trays with buttered paper.
7. Spoon the mixture on to the tray with a small teaspoon leaving a gap of about 5cm/2in round each one. For *petits fours* use about ⅓ of a teaspoon. You may find you will have to cook these biscuits in two batches.
8. Place the trays on shelves near the centre of the oven.
9. Cook for 10-12 minutes in the oven, until they turn a dark golden brown.
10. Take the biscuits out of the oven and lift them from the tray using a fishslice. Put the biscuits on a cake-rack and leave to cool.

To use for presents, pack the biscuits in a small plastic bag and tie the bag up with a gay ribbon.

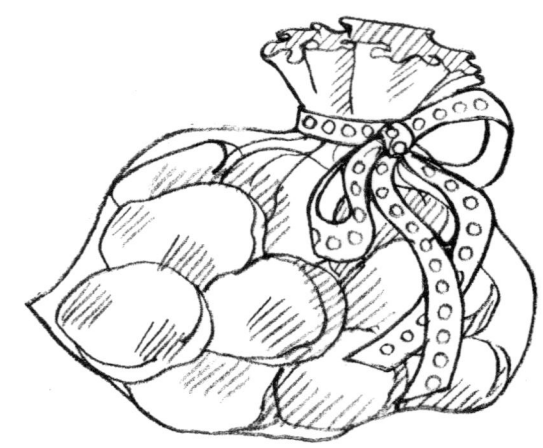

Ginger is a native of tropical Asia and the tuberous root is part of the plant we eat. It is used fresh or dried and can also be preserved in syrup or crystallized. It is a very important ingredient in the making of Indian curry but in European cookery it is mainly used in powdered form in puddings, cakes and biscuits.

Cakes for Special People

It is very useful to have a recipe for a basic cake which can be flavoured and coloured in any way you like. It can be cooked either in an oblong bread tin or a round sandwich tin or deep cake tin depending on your plans for the decoration and the number of people you wish to feed.

Cooking Guide for Basic Cake

Pre-heat the oven to moderate (180°C, 350°F, Mark 4).

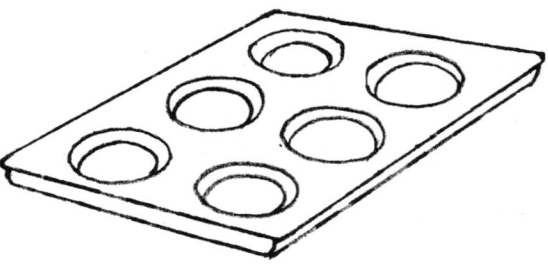

Buns about 25 minutes in a patty tin.

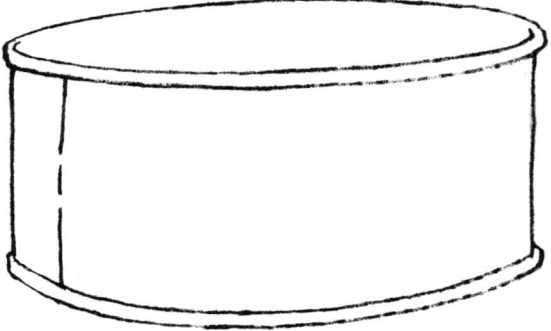

Cake tin 18cm/7in diameter, 7½cm/3in depth, about 1½ hours.

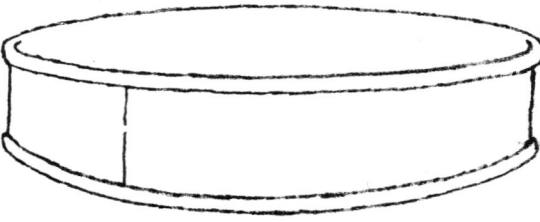

Sandwich tin 18cm/7in diameter, 2½cm/1in depth, about 40 minutes.

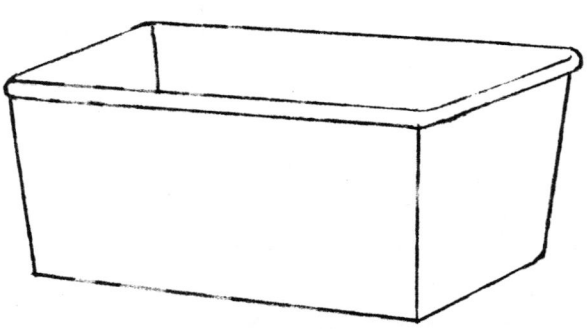

Oblong 400g/1lb bread tin 18½cm/7½in length, 10cm/4in depth, about 50 minutes.

Basic Cake

Ingredients
100g (4oz) margarine or butter
100g (4oz) sugar
1 egg
125g (5oz) self-raising flour*
2-5 tablespoons milk or fruit juice
* If you use plain flour add 1½ level teaspoons baking powder

Flavours
Chocolate: add 3 tablespoons cocoa.
Lemon: use the grated zest of half a lemon and 1 tablespoon of lemon juice.
Orange: use the grated zest of a small orange and 2 tablespoons of orange juice.
Plain cake: add 2-3 drops of vanilla essence. If you are doubling the basic ingredients to make the large cake you will also have to double the amount of flavouring.

Colouring
Add the red, green or other edible food colouring a drop at a time. Mix well so that the cake mixture is coloured evenly all over.

Tools
mixing bowl, fork, wooden spoon, cake or bread tin, sieve, cup, greaseproof paper, cake rack, knife, scissors, buttered paper, oven gloves

Method
1 Pre-heat the oven to moderate (180°C, 350°F, Mark 4).
2 Line the bottom of the cake or bread tin with a piece of greaseproof paper. Grease the tin and the paper lightly to prevent the cake sticking.
3 Put the margarine or butter in a bowl with the sugar. Stir and beat with a fork. This is called creaming, because when the mixture is ready it looks rather like very thick cream. If the fat is soft this will take about 2-3 minutes.
4 Beat the egg in a cup with a fork.
5 Add the beaten egg to the butter and sugar mixture and beat thoroughly.
6 Sieve the flour into a basin, adding the baking powder if you are using plain flour.
7 Fold half the flour into the egg and butter mixture, stir it in and then beat with a wooden spoon.
8 Add the rest of the flour and the cocoa powder if you are making a chocolate cake. Stir and beat again with a wooden spoon.
9 Add the milk, grated zest, fruit juice or edible food colouring or a mixture of these until the cake mixture drops easily if you give the spoon a tiny shake—be careful that the mixture is not too liquid or the cake will not rise!
10 Put the cake mixture in the middle of the tin and spread it evenly with a spoon.
11 Put the cake on the middle shelf in the oven and cook according to the time chart.
12 To find out whether it is cooked stick a knife through the centre of the cake. If it comes out clean the cake is cooked. The cake will also tend to shrink away a little from the sides of the tin when it is ready.
13 Once the cake is cooked take it out of the oven. Allow it to cool before removing it from the tin and placing it on a cake rack.

Water Icing

Once the basic cake is cooked the fun can really begin. There are recipes for water icing and butter icing. These can be flavoured in exactly the same way as the cake. Add a little colouring or flavouring and check it for taste. You may find it tempting when it comes to butter icing to do rather more tasting than is absolutely necessary, so include a little extra butter and sugar for this purpose!

Ingredients
300g (¾lb) icing sugar
3-3½ tablespoons water or fruit juice

For piping decorations use half the above ingredients. 300g/¾lb icing sugar is enough to cover a sandwich cake with a 17½cm/7in diameter. For a large cake allow 400g/1lb icing sugar. Unless you are an expert at decorating cakes it is a good idea to be a little extravagant with the icing sugar!

Tools
basin, sieve, tablespoon, icing syringe or greaseproof-paper funnel, wooden board or meat plate, knife with rounded end, kettle or saucepan, jug, oven gloves

Method
1 Sieve the icing sugar into a basin.
2 Slowly add either the water, fruit juice, edible food colouring or a mixture of these, to the icing sugar. For a chocolate icing you will need about 1 tablespoon cocoa.
3 Mix the icing sugar to a smooth, stiff paste. If the mixture becomes thin add more icing sugar to thicken it.
4 Boil about 1 litre/1¾ pints of water in a kettle or saucepan and pour it into a jug.
5 To ice the cake place it on a wooden board, or a plate, turned upside down.
6 Spoon the water icing on to the top of the cake in the centre. Spread it evenly over the top and down the sides using a knife with a rounded end. Dip the knife into the basin of hot water sometimes; a warmed knife makes the icing spread more easily.

Butter Icing

Ingredients
50g (2oz) butter
75g (3oz) 6 tablespoons icing
   or granulated sugar
Vanilla essence or 1-3 teaspoons
   fruit juice for flavouring
Choose granulated sugar if you like a crunchy icing or icing sugar if you want a really smooth butter icing.

Tools
basin, fork, knife with a rounded end, teaspoon, tablespoon

Method
1. Put the butter in a basin and soften by beating it with a fork. It helps to put the butter in a warm place before you start, but take care that it does not melt!

2. Add the sugar a little at a time and beat it in well until the mixture becomes creamy. This can be quite hard work.

3. To flavour the butter icing mix in 2 drops of vanilla essence or 1-3 teaspoons orange or lemon juice. To colour it add one or two drops of edible food colouring and beat it in well. Alternatively 1-3 teaspoons of cocoa or coffee essence can be added. If you use instant coffee powder, dissolve 1 teaspoon powder in 2 teaspoons hot water. Add gradually to prevent it from curdling.

Butter icing can either be used as a cake filling or be spread over the top of the cake instead of water icing. If you are using it for both add an extra 25g/1oz butter and 40g/1½oz sugar.

Smiler

The cake recipe appears on *page 73* and the instructions for water icing and butter icing on *pages 74, 75*.

Ingredients
1 sandwich cake
200g (½lb) water icing for the cake
125g (5oz) butter icing

Tools
large sharp knife, chopping board or plate upside-down, knife with a blunt edge, jug for hot water, icing syringe or greaseproof-paper funnel

Method

1 Cut the cake in half to form two circles.

2 Spread the butter icing evenly over one half. Leave a little in the bowl to use to fill in any gaps which appear at the edge of the cake when the two halves are put together.

3 Put the two halves of the cake together, and fill in any gaps at the edge as this will make the cake easier to ice.

4 Ice the cake *page 74*, and leave to dry. Leave a little icing in the bowl to use for marking out the Smiler. Add a few drops of edible food colouring to this. If the icing hardens while the cake icing is drying place the bowl over a pan of simmering water for a minute to soften it.

5 When the icing covering the cake is nearly dry mark out a Smiler face using an icing syringe or a greaseproof-paper funnel.

Cottage

Ingredients
2 oblong cakes
250g (10oz) chocolate butter icing
300g (¾lb) chocolate water icing
4 lumps sugar
Silver balls
Sugared flowers or petals
Chocolate flake bar or 50g/2oz chocolate

If you are unable to obtain all the above items try to think of something which will do in their place. Crystallized cherries, for instance, cut up, could be used instead of the sugared flowers or petals, and Smarties, although a little big, could be used for the windows and doors.

Tools
large sharp knife, chopping board or plate upside-down, knife with a blunt edge, jug for hot water, icing syringe or greaseproof-paper funnel

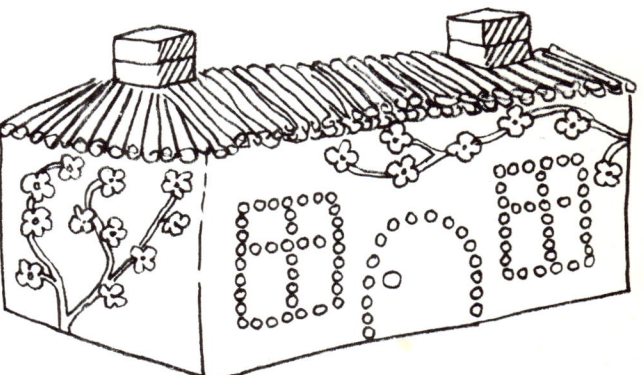

Method
1 Cut the top off one of the cakes to make the surface even.
2 Spread a third of the butter icing over this flat surface.
3 Put the other cake on top and fill in any gaps at the sides using some of the butter icing.
4 Pile the remaining butter icing on top of the cake and shape it to form a sloping roof.
5 Place two lumps of sugar at each end of the roof to form chimneys.
6 Cover the chimneys, roof and sides of the cottage with chocolate water icing, *page 74.*
7 Before the icing hardens mark out the windows and door with silver balls. Arrange the sugared flowers or petals round the windows and doors. Do not forget the door knocker.
8 Carefully cut the flake chocolate bar or the chocolate into thin strips with a knife so that it looks like straw. Cover the roof of the cottage with this to resemble thatch.

Maypole

Ingredients
1 large round cake
250g (10oz) butter icing
400g (1lb) water icing
Hundreds-and-thousands
3.3m/3yd gift-wrap ribbon
 about 1-1½cm/½in wide
1 stick of peppermint rock
 about 23cm/9in long
Sellotape

Tools
large sharp knife, chopping board or plate upside-down, knife with a blunt edge, jug for hot water, icing syringe or greaseproof-paper funnel

Method
1 Cut the cake so that you have three layers.

2 Cover two of the layers with butter icing. Leave plenty of butter icing in the bowl to fill in any gaps which appear at the side of the cake when it is put together again. It is impossible to ice a big cake unless the sides are perfect and straight.

3 Put the layers one on top of the other and fill in any gaps with butter icing.

4 Cover with coloured water icing, *page 74*. Decorate with hundreds-and-thousands.

5 Wrap a piece of ribbon round the stick of rock, and hold it in place with Sellotape top and bottom. Stick the piece of rock in the middle of the cake. It should go in to a depth of about 5cm/2in.

6 Cut the ribbon in four 61cm/24in lengths and one 30½cm/12in length.

7 Lay one ribbon at a time over the top of the stick of rock, allowing an equal length to hang down on each side. Twist and secure to the cake on both sides with the damp icing. Repeat this until four ribbons have been evenly placed round the cake and held in position with water icing. Tie the ribbons tother on top of the rock with the remaining length of ribbon, this will prevent the others sliding off.

The Smiler and the Cottage can be turned into birthday cakes by adding candles. It is not safe to light candles on the Maypole cake as the ribbons might catch fire.

Ice-Cream Cake

If the freezer section of your refrigerator is deep enough to take a small cake tin or if you have a deep freeze you could make an ice-cream cake. Remember to use only a plastic or tin container or ovenproof porcelain in a deep freeze. The tin should be about 6½cm/2¾in deep and have a diameter of about 15cm/6in. It should be able to hold 1 litre/1¾ pints of liquid. Ice-cream cakes are good for birthdays and look very pretty lit with candles. They require no cooking and are easy to put together.

Ingredients
250ml (½ pint) double cream
8 level tablespoons icing sugar
4 eggs
Red and green edible food colouring*
Hundreds-and-thousands
* The colours are only suggestions; you can use any others you like.

Tools
egg beater, tablespoon, 2 basins, cake tin or soufflé dish, spoon, fork, tinfoil, kettle, baking tin, oven gloves

Method
1 Prepare a piece of tinfoil which is large enough to wrap up the tin or soufflé dish in which you are making the ice-cream cake.
2 Turn to *page 41* and follow the instructions for vanilla ice-cream.
3 When the mixture is ready to freeze put it in two separate basins.
4 Add red edible food colouring to the mixture in one basin to make it pink, and add green colouring to the other.
5 Using a fork, blend the colouring thoroughly into the mixture in each basin.
6 Put the pink ice-cream mixture in the bottom of the tin or soufflé dish. Smooth the surface flat with a spoon, add the green mixture and smooth again.
7 Sit the tin or dish on the tinfoil, cover it over, and place it in the freezer section of your refrigerator or in a deep freeze. Allow to set firm overnight.
8 Bring about 1½ litres/2½ pints of water to boil in a kettle.
9 Take the ice-cream out of the freezer. Unwrap the tinfoil, smooth it out and keep it ready for further use.
10 Pour the boiling water into a baking tin, filling it to a depth of about 2½cm/1in.
11 Set the tin or dish in the hot water for about ½ minute so that the bottom of the ice-cream melts enough to turn it out. Turn the ice-cream on to the tinfoil.
12 The cake can be decorated at this stage with hundreds-and-thousands. You must be quick otherwise the cake will melt away! And it is dangerous to re-freeze ice-cream.
13 Cover the decorated cake well with tinfoil but keep it clear of the top of the cake so that the decoration is not spoilt. Put the cake back in the freezer section of your refrigerator or in the deep freeze. If you are keeping it in a deep freeze you will probably need to take it out 20 minutes before you want to cut it as it will be very hard. Stick the candle holders into the cake at this point.

Vegetables

It is very important not to overcook vegetables, especially green vegetables. If they have to be kept hot, root vegetables such as carrots and turnips are a much better choice than green vegetables such as brussels sprouts and green cabbage, which are only really delicious when eaten straight from the stove. For this reason winter and summer salads make useful alternatives to hot vegetables and can perfectly easily be served with hot food, though if you do this it is a good idea to serve them on side-plates. From a health point of view salads are excellent as vegetables tend to lose some of their mineral salt and vitamin value while they are cooking.

All vegetables should be washed in salted water and drained well in a colander or sieve before cooking. There are many different ways to cook vegetables but you will not go very far wrong if you use the method described here. Spinach is an exception and should be cooked without any water other than that clinging to the leaves after washing.

Vegetables can be served tossed in butter. Put about 15g (½oz) butter in the serving dish, add the vegetables and place a lid on the dish. Give the dish several good shakes and the vegetables will be covered with butter. For vegetables served with a white sauce see the recipe on *page 36* and leave out the cheese.

Method

1. Put enough water in a saucepan to cover the vegetable you are cooking.
2. Put the saucepan on the heat and bring the water to the boil.
3. Add the vegetables and ¼ teaspoon of salt.
4. Bring the water back to the boil, turn down the heat and simmer.

A guide to the preparation and cooking time for vegetables is given here.

Tools

large bowl, chopping board, knife, kitchen scissors, teaspoon, colander or sieve, saucepan, oven gloves

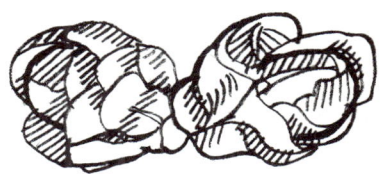

Vegetable	Preparation	Approximate cooking time
Broccoli	Remove the thicker part of the stalk, then cut a cross at the base of each to speed up the cooking time.	8-10 minutes
Broad Beans	Remove the beans from the pods. The length of cooking time will depend on age and size. Serve either with white sauce or tossed in butter and chopped parsley.	15-20 minutes
Brussels sprouts	Remove any damaged leaves and trim the stalks if necessary.	5-8 minutes
Cabbage	Remove any damaged leaves and shred finely with a pair of kitchen scissors or a sharp knife.	
	Green Cabbage	4-5 minutes
	White cabbage	8 minutes
Carrots	Baby carrots should be scrubbed well and cooked whole, after removing the stalks and leaves.	15 minutes
	Old carrots should be scraped and in some cases peeled. They taste delicious if they are sliced almost as finely as cucumber and they cook very quickly this way.	10 minutes
Cauliflower	Throw away the larger green leaves. Trim the stalk and cut a deep cross at the base—this is important otherwise the flower part may become overcooked while you are waiting for the stem to become tender. Make sure the saucepan you choose is deep enough to hold sufficient water to cover the cauliflower. Serve with a white sauce.	20-25 minutes
Green Peas	Remove the pods. The cooking time will depend very much on the size and age of the peas. Put some mint in the cooking water and serve tossed in butter.	5-10 minutes

		Approximate cooking time
Leeks	Shorten the green tops to about 6cm/2-3in and cut off the roots. Clean under running water. If the leeks are very muddy you may have to open up the outer leaves to remove the earth. With medium and large sized leeks it will probably be necessary to remove the outside layer. Leeks should be drained well before serving. Cover with white sauce. Cooking time depends on size.	30-40 minutes
	Young leeks and leeks cut in 2cm/¾in lengths.	20-30 minutes
New Potatoes	Scrub and scrape new potatoes and add a sprig of mint to the cooking water.	10-20 minutes
Old Potatoes	Peel the skins from old potatoes. The cooking time will depend on the size so cut each in 4-6 pieces if you are in a hurry.	20-30 minutes
	Chips and roast potatoes taste very good, but leave these for an adult to cook. Few things are more dangerous than hot fat. Baked potatoes, *page 90*.	
Runner beans	Top and tail. Remove the stringy edge by taking a very thin slice off all the way round. Either cut diagonally or from end to end in thin slices.	5-8 minutes
Spinach	This has to be washed very carefully and it can be a tiresome job. The tough stalks and damaged parts of the leaves should be thrown away. Cook the damp leaves without adding water.	7-8 minutes
Turnips	These are cleaned like carrots. If they are young, scrub and scrape them; if they are old peel them.	
	Young, sliced	5-10 minutes
	Old, sliced	10-15 minutes

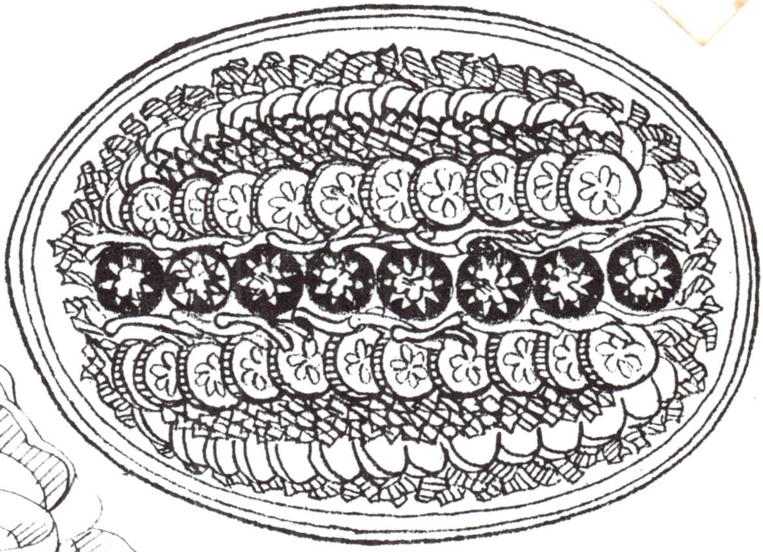

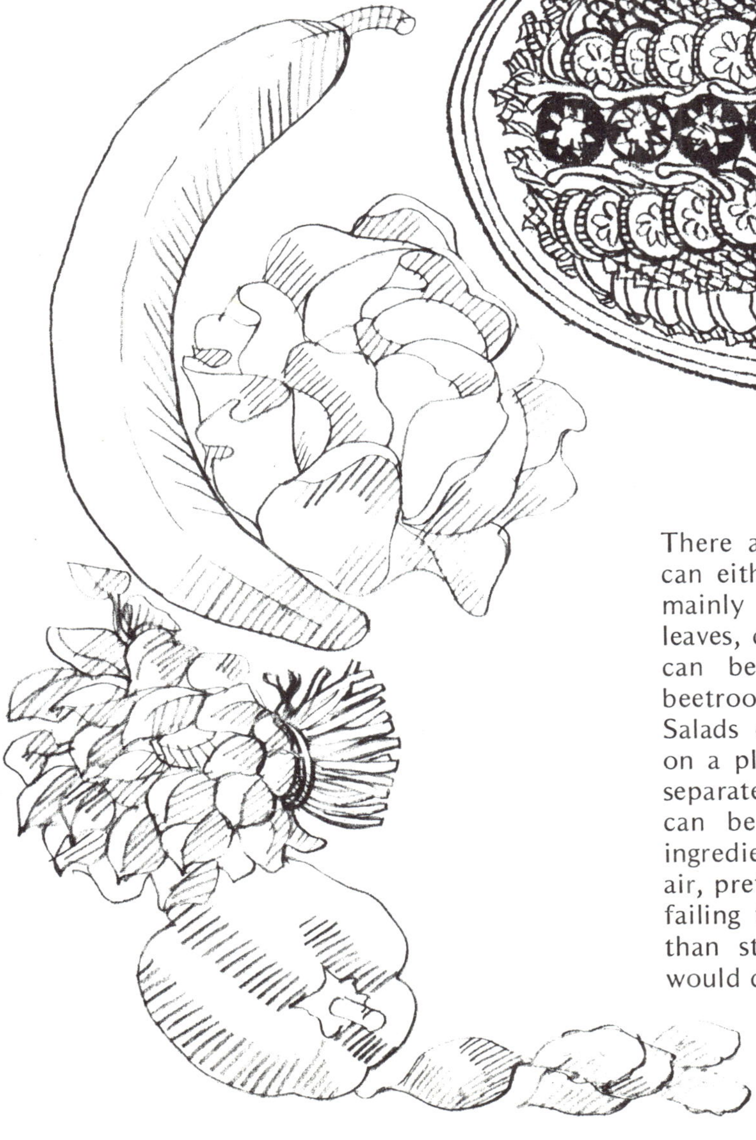

There are two basic summer salads, they can either be green, which means sticking mainly to watercress, lettuce, spinach leaves, cucumber and green pepper or they can be mixed, in which case radishes, beetroot and tomatoes can all be added. Salads can either be arranged attractively on a plate, with all the ingredients placed separately in neat rows or circles, or they can be tossed. For a tossed salad the ingredients should be lightly lifted in the air, preferably with wooden salad servers or failing that with a spoon and fork, rather than stirred heavily with a spoon which would damage the green leaves.

Summer salads

Tossed Mixed Salad

Ingredients Serves 4
8-12 lettuce leaves
8 sprigs watercress
2 tomatoes
10cm/4in length of cucumber
4-5 radishes
Chives, mint or parsley
A few spring onions
3 tablespoons vinaigrette dressing

Tools
salad basket or clean tea cloth, knife, chopping board, salad servers or spoon and fork, salad bowl

If you have not got all the ingredients above it does not matter, just add an extra amount of the items available. You may notice that beetroot is not on the list. The juice runs easily and would make the rest of the ingredients spotted pink and messy looking, so serve it separately in a dish.

Method
1 Wash the lettuce leaves and watercress carefully in salt and water. Dry them thoroughly by shaking them in a special salad basket or by patting them gently with a clean tea towel.
2 Cut the cucumber in very thin slices. If you have the time sprinkle it with a little salt and leave to stand for a few minutes so that some of the juice runs out.
3 Wash the tomatoes and either quarter them or cut in thin, round slices.
4 Scrub the radishes clean and cut off their roots and tops. Also wash the spring onions, cutting off their roots and trimming the stems to leave about 10cm/4in.
5 Chop the chives, mint or parsley.
6 Put about three tablespoons of vinaigrette dressing, *page 87* in a salad bowl and mix in the chives, mint or parsley.
7 Just before serving add the rest of the ingredients and toss lightly with salad servers or with a spoon or fork. This must be done at the last minute as the lettuce will become limp if left in the vinaigrette dressing for too long.

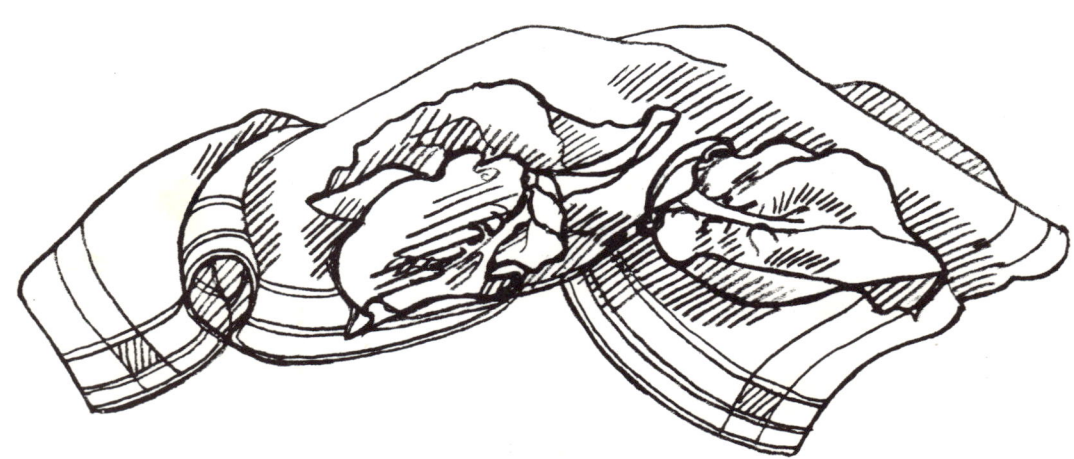

Summer salads

Arranged Salad

Ingredients Serves 4
2 tomatoes
4 spring onions
4 cooked new potatoes
1 beetroot
6-8 lettuce leaves
7½-10cm/(3-4in) cucumber
Chives, mint or parsley
2 tablespoons mayonnaise or
 salad cream

Tools
meat dish, chopping board, kitchen scissors, sharp knife, salad basket or clean tea cloth, spoon

Method

1. Cut the beetroot into ½cm/¼in cubes.
2. Wash the lettuce and dry, *page 84*. Roll the lettuce leaves up loosely and cut into strips ½cm/¼in wide with a pair of kitchen scissors or a knife.
3. Wash the spring onions, cutting off the roots and the stems to leave about 10cm/4in.
4. Chop the chives, mint or parsley.
5. Cut the cucumber in thin slices.
6. Turn the tomatoes into water-lilies by cutting a series of continuous 'V' shapes round the tomato with a sharp knife until they meet. Next lift the tops off the tomatoes, they will come away easily with the help of a knife.
7. Slice the new potatoes in thin slices.
8. Place the tomatoes in a line down the centre of a meat dish. Decorate the tomato centres with mayonnaise or salad cream. Slip the spring onions between the tomato halves keeping two for the centre of the row.
9. Put a row of cucumber on each side of the tomatoes, then a row of beetroot next to the cucumber. The potatoes follow next and then the lettuce.
10. Sprinkle the potatoes with chopped chives, parsley or mint.

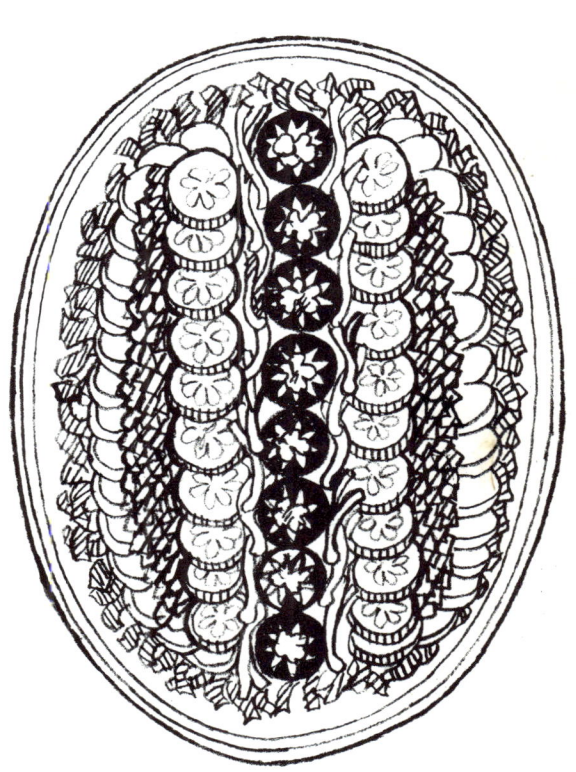

Winter Salad with Chedder Cheese

Ingredients
150g (6oz) Cheddar cheese
150g (6oz) white cabbage
    (makes 3 teacupfuls)
100g (4oz) carrots (makes
    2 teacupfuls)
4 sticks of celery
    (makes 2 teacupfuls)
2 small beetroot (makes
    1 teacupful)
2 tablespoons onion
    (½ small onion)
2 tablespoons sauce vinaigrette
4 tablespoons sultanas
Pepper and ¼ teaspoon salt
Sprigs of parsley

Serves 4

Tools
grater, chopping board, sharp knife, kitchen scissors, teacup, salad bowl, tablespoon, teaspoon

Method
1 Shred the cabbage with kitchen scissors or a sharp knife.
2 Scrape the carrots and grate them.
3 Grate the onion or chop finely.
4 Chop the celery and beetroot into small cubes about 1cm/½in wide.
5 Grate the cheese.
6 Mix the cabbage, carrot, onion, celery, beetroot, sultanas, vinaigrette, salt and a shake of pepper together in a salad bowl.
7 Make a hollow in the centre of the mixture of vegetables and fill this with the grated cheese.
8 Dot the cheese with small sprigs of parsley.

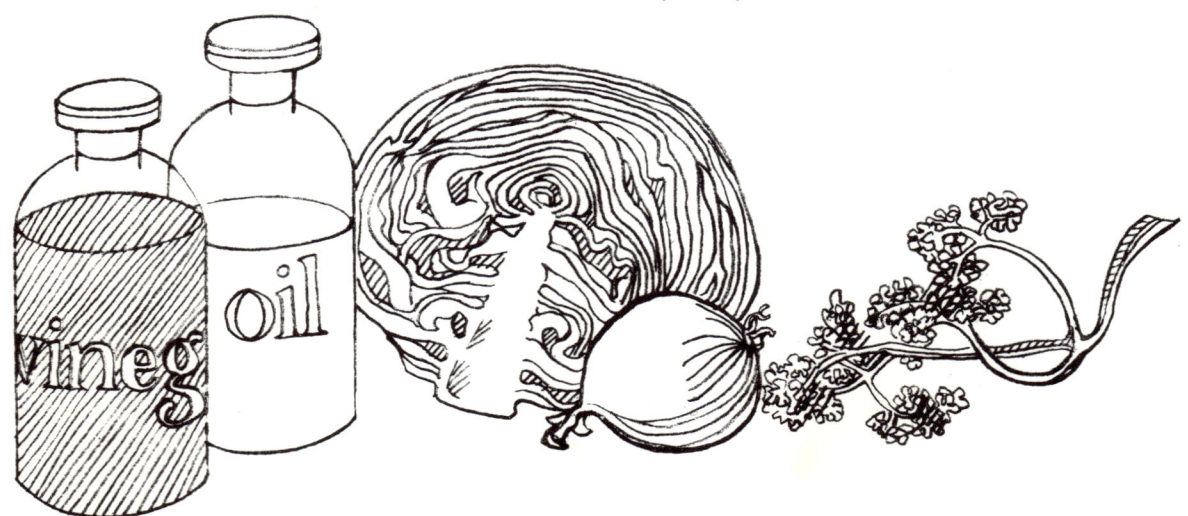

Vinaigrette Dressing

Ingredients
2 tablespoons olive or corn oil
2 teaspoons vinegar
Pinch of dry mustard
2 shakes of pepper
Pinch of garlic salt or plain salt

Some people add sugar to sauce vinaigrette so if you are not using garlic salt try ¼ teaspoon sugar and see if you like the sweet taste.

Tools
bowl, tablespoon, wooden spoon

Method
1 Put the vinegar in bowl and add the mustard, salt and pepper. Stir thoroughly.
2 Add the olive or corn oil and stir again.

The above is enough for a tossed salad for 4 people. If you are serving the vinaigrette dressing in a jug, make at least treble the above quantity. It can be stored afterwards in a bottle with a screw top.

Mayonnaise

Ingredients
2 egg yolks
250ml (½ pint) olive or corn oil
2-3 teaspoons lemon juice or
 vinegar, or a mixture of both
Salt and pepper
A little dry mustard (this is not essential)

Method
1 Separate the yolks from the whites of egg, *page 33*. Put the yolks in a small basin and the whites in a covered container to use later for meringues or ice-cream.
2 Put the oil in a small jug with a good pouring lip.
3 Add one teaspoonful of lemon juice or vinegar to the egg yolks; also add the salt, pepper and dry mustard. Blend these ingredients well together by stirring them with a wooden spoon for 1 minute.

Tools
small basin, small jug, wooden spoon, teaspoon, measuring cup

4 Hold the jug with the oil in it in your left hand and continue to stir the egg yolk mixture with your right hand. Add the oil drop by drop while you stir. It is extremely important not to add the oil too quickly, or the oil and egg will separate.
5 After 10 minutes the mixture should start to thicken. You can then pour the oil out of the jug in a steady stream.
6 Add the rest of the vinegar or lemon juice, taste and add more salt and pepper if necessary.

If the oil and egg separate while you are making the mayonnaise, start again by using 1 egg yolk and 1 teaspoon of lemon juice or vinegar. Stir the egg and lemon juice or vinegar together for 1 minute; then very slowly pour on the separated mayonnaise stirring all the time with the other hand.

Stuffed Eggs

Ingredients
4 eggs
2 tablespoons grated Cheddar
    cheese
2 tablespoons mayonnaise or
    1 tablespoon salad cream
1 spring onion or small
    piece of onion
Salt and pepper
Sprigs of parsley for decoration

Serves 4

Tools
saucepan, grater, basin,
chopping board, knife,
tablespoon, teaspoon, fork,
oven gloves

Method
1 Hard-boil the eggs by cooking them in boiling water for 10 minutes, *page 55*.
2 As soon as the eggs are cooked pour off the boiling water and refill the saucepan with cold water. Be careful not to burn yourself.
3 Keep the eggs in cold water until they are cool and then remove the shells.
4 Chop the onion into very fine pieces.
5 Cut the eggs in half and gently remove the yolks with a teaspoon without breaking the whites. Put the yolks in a basin.
6 Grate the cheese.
7 Add the mayonnaise or salad cream to the egg yolk and also the cheese, onion, salt and a shake of pepper. Mix all these ingredients together with a fork.
8 Pile this mixture back into the egg halves and decorate with sprigs of parsley.

Serve the stuffed eggs on either a bed of lettuce leaves or shredded white cabbage.

To eat with salads

Stuffed Tomatoes

Ingredients
4 large tomatoes
1 tin tuna fish (99g/3½oz)
2 small sticks celery
2 tablespoons mayonnaise or
   1 tablespoon salad cream
Salt and pepper
Sprigs of parsley or mint
   for decoration

Serves 4

Tools
knife, basin, tablespoon, tin opener, fork, chopping board

Method
1. Cut the tomatoes in half and carefully scrape out the seeds. Put the seeds and pulp into a basin.
2. Open the tin of tuna fish.
3. Cut the celery in very small pieces about ½cm/¼-½in square.
4. Add the tuna fish, celery, mayonnaise or salad dressing to the tomato pulp and also add a pinch of salt and a shake of pepper. Mix all the ingredients together thoroughly with a fork. Taste and add more salt and pepper if necessary.
5. Pile the mixture into the tomato shells and decorate with parsley or mint.

Stuffed Jacket Potatoes

Ingredients Serves 4
- 4 large potatoes
- 100g (4oz) grated cheese *or*
  - 1 tin (124g/4¾oz) sardines *or*
  - 1 tin (227g/8oz) pilchards in tomato sauce
- 2 tablespoons milk
- 50g (2oz) butter
- 4 tablespoons dried breadcrumbs
- Salt and pepper

Tools
scrubbing brush, tea cloth, grater, baking tray, fork, tin opener, chopping board, knife, tablespoon, basin, oven gloves

Method

To Bake Potatoes

1. Scrub the potatoes, cut out any 'eyes' and damaged parts and dry with a cloth.
2. Prick the potatoes with a fork to prevent them bursting while they are cooking.
3. Put the potatoes on a baking tray and cook them in a moderate oven (170°-180°C, 325°-350°F, Mark 3-4) for 1½ to 2 hours.
4. Squeeze the potatoes with your hand in an oven glove and if they feel soft then they are cooked.

Stuffed Potatoes

5. Remove the potatoes from the oven and cut them in half on a chopping board. Scoop out the cooked potato with a spoon and put it in a basin.
6. Add half the butter, the milk, a pinch of salt and a shake of pepper and the cheese, or sardines or pilchards. Mash the mixture well together with a fork.
7. Light a gas grill or switch on an electric one.
8. Spoon the potato mixture back into the skins, sprinkle half a tablespoon of breadcrumbs over each one. Divide the remaining butter into 8 pieces and put a piece on each stuffed potato.
9. Put the potatoes under a hot grill for 5 minutes to brown the top and warm the potato through.

To eat with salads

Garlic Bread

Ingredients
1 medium-sized French loaf
3 cloves garlic
100g (¼lb) butter

Serves 4

Tools
chopping board, garlic squeezer or small knife, bread knife, small saucepan, tinfoil, oven gloves

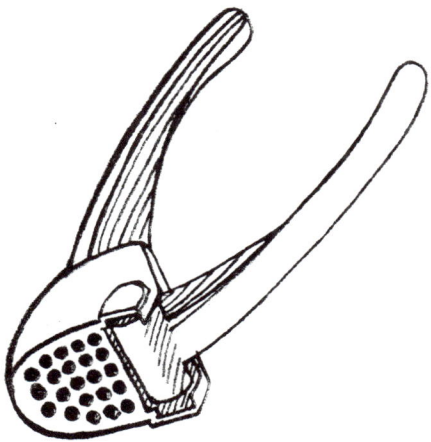

Method

1. Pre-heat the oven to fairly hot (190°C, 375°F, Mark 5).
2. Peel the skin off the garlic cloves and either crush them in a garlic squeezer or cut them in thin slices and flatten with a knife.
3. Melt the butter in a saucepan on a low heat. Add the garlic.
4. While the butter is slowly melting, slice the French bread. Take care not to cut all the way through so that the slices are held together by the bottom crust.
5. Place the French bread on a piece of tinfoil.
6. Slightly open up the cut slices and pour a little melted garlic butter between each slice.
7. Wrap the tinfoil over the bread and put it in the oven for 20 minutes.

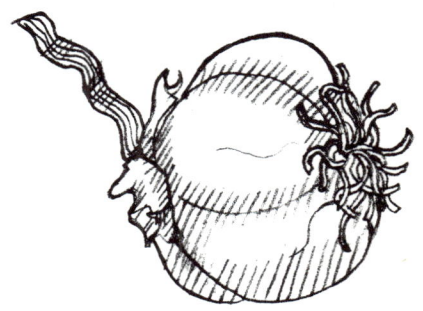

Garlic has a very strong flavour and should be used sparingly. The recipe above uses a considerable amount of garlic and will only appeal to garlic lovers! The bulb is the part we eat and it is made up of several cloves. Garlic is also available in powdered form but this is a poor substitute for the real thing.

Index

American egg sandwiches, 55
Apples, toffee, 66
Arranged salad, 85

Bananas, baked, 39
    with ham, 36
Barbecued Frankfurters, 59
    Hamburgers, 59
Barbecue sauces, hot, 60
    sweet, 60
Basil, 29
Batter, 44
Bay leaves, 22
Beans, runner, 82
Birthday cake, *see cottage or smiler cake*
Biscuits, chocolate Krispies, 69
    crunchy ginger, 70
    Rice Krispie boats, 69
    vanilla, 68
Boiled eggs, 17
Brandy snap slices, 37
Breadcrumbs, 48
Bread, garlic, 91
Bread sauce, 21
Broad beans, 81
Broccoli, 81
Brussels sprouts, 81
Butter icing, 74

Cabbage, 81
Cake, basic birthday, 73, *see cottage or smiler cake*
    chocolate biscuit, 26
    cottage, 77
    ice-cream, 79
    maypole, 78
    smiler, 76
Caramel toast, 61
Carrots, 81
Cauliflower, 81
Charlotte's fruit milk jelly, 52
Cheese and onion flan, 34
Cheese, Cheddar salad, 86
Cheese rolls, Rupert's, 56
Cheese sauce, 36
Cherry flan, 50
Chicken, honey brown, 20

Chocolate biscuit cake, 26
    Krispies, 69
    mandarin orange trifle, 30
    queen's pudding, 48
Cinnamon, 63
    toast, 63
Coffee crumble, 33
    'Instant', 19
    real, 18
Cottage cake, 77
Crunchy ginger biscuits, 70
Curried eggs, 42
Curry powder, 43
Curry sauce, 42

Egg nests, 57
Eggs and bacon, 16
Eggs, boiled, 17
    curried, 42
    hard boiled, 55
Egg sandwiches, American, 55
Eggs, stuffed, 88

Flan case pastry, 50
Flan, cherry, 50
Flan, cheese and onion, 34
Frankfurters, barbecued, 59
French toast, 62
Fruit ice-cream, 41
Fudge, Garnett, 65

Garlic, 91
Garlic bread, 91
Garnett fudge, 65
Ginger, 70
Ginger biscuits, 70
Gooseberry snow, 24
Gravy, basic, 22
Green peas, 81

Hamburgers, barbecued, 59
Ham with bananas, 36

Ice-cream cake, 79
    fruit, 41
    vanilla, 41
Iced syllabub, 23

Index

Icing, butter, 74
    water, 74

Jelly, Charlotte's fruit milk, 52

Kedgeree, 45

Leeks, 82

Macaroni cheese, 46
Mayonnaise, 87
Maypole cake, 78
Meat loaf, 32
Meringues, 33
Miranda's jam pancakes, 44

Omelette, saucy, 49
Onion soup, 27
Oranges in syrup, 35

Pancakes, Miranda's jam, 44
    traditional, 44
Pastry flan case, 50
Pastry, shortcrust, 50
Peppermint creams, 67
Potatoes, 82
    baked, 90
    stuffed jacket, 90

Queen's pudding, chocolate, 48

Rhubarb snow, 24
Rice, 53
Rice Krispie boats, 69
Risotto, 38
Runner beans, 82
Rupert's cheese rolls, 56

Salads, 83
    arranged, 85
    tossed mixed, 84
    winter, 86
Sandwiches, American egg, 55
Sauce, barbecue, hot, 60
    sweet, 60
    bread, 21
    cheese, 36
    curry, 42
    soy, 38
Saucy omelette, 49
Scones, fruit, 25
    plain, 25
Smiler cake, 76
Snow, gooseberry, 24
    rhubarb, 24
Soup, onion, 27
Soy sauce, 38
Spaghetti, 29
Spaghetti Bolognese, 28
Spinach, 82
Stuffed eggs, 88
    jacket potatoes, 90
    tomatoes, 89
Syllabub, iced, 23

Tea, 19
Thyme, 32
Toad-in-the-hole, 40
Toast, 17
    caramel, 61
    cinnamon, 63
    French, 62
Toffee apples, 66
Tomatoes, stuffed, 89
Trifle, chocolate mandarin orange, 30
Turnips, 82

Vanilla biscuits, 68
    ice-cream, 41
Vegetables, 80
Vinaigrette dressing, 87

Water icing, 74
Winter salad with Cheddar cheese, 86

Oven Temperatures

heat of oven	thermostat settings	approximate electrical oven temperatures '°F'	'°C'
very cool	¼	225	110
very cool	½	250	130
cool	1	275	140
cool	2	300	150
moderate	3	325	170
moderate	4	350	180
fairly hot	5	375	190
fairly hot	6	400	200
hot	7	425	220
very hot	8	450	230
very hot	9	475	240

Reproduced with permission from the Gas Council.

Useful Measures

1 teacupful = 200ml/⅓ pint/13 tablespoons

2 crustless slices bread equal about 50g/2oz = 1 teacupful

1 teacupful rice = 125g/5oz

1 teacupful sugar = 150g/6oz   1 level tablespoonful = 15g/½oz

1 teacupful icing sugar = 100g/4oz   1 level tablespoonful = 10g/⅓oz

1 teacupful flour = 100g/4oz   1 level tablespoonful = 10g/⅓oz

1 teacupful shredded cabbage or grated carrot = about 50g/2oz

1 teacupful demerara sugar = 125g/5oz